calculations for HOSPITALITY & CATERING

D1427638

GORDON E GEE

Formerly Head of Department of
Food and Fashion,
South Downs College of Further Education, Havant,
Hants

Formerly Examiner in Book-keeping and Food costing
for the East Midlands Educational Union

Member of the West Sussex Valuation Tribunal

Hodder & Stoughton
A MEMBER OF THE HODDER HEADLINE GROUP

Orders: Please contact Bookpoint Ltd, 130 Milton Park, Abingdon, Oxon OX14 4SB. Telephone: (44) 01235 400414, Fax: (44) 01235 400454. Lines are open from 9 am - 6 pm, Monday to Saturday, with a 24-hour message answering service. Email address: orders@bookpoint.co.uk

British Library Cataloguing in Publication Data
A catalogue record for this title is available from The British Library

ISBN 0–340–683457

First published 1980
Second edition 1989
Third edition 1997

Impression number 11 10 9 8 7 6 5 4
Year 2005 2004 2003 2002 2001

Copyright © 1980, 1989, 1997, G. E. Gee

All rights reserved. No part of this publication may be reproduced or transmitted in any form or by any means, electronic or mechanical, including photocopy, recording, or any information storage and retrieval system, without permission in writing from the publisher or under licence from the Copyright Licensing Agency Limited. Further details of such licences (for reprographic reproduction) may be obtained from the Copyright Licensing Agency Limited, of 90 Tottenham Court Road, London W1P 0LP.

Typeset by Wearset, Boldon, Tyne and Wear.
Printed in Great Britain for Hodder & Stoughton Educational, a division of Hodder Headline Plc, 338 Euston Road, London NW1 3BH, by
The Bath Press, Bath

Preface

BRIDGEND COLLEGE
LIBRARY

In writing this book both students and lecturers have been kept constantly in mind. To achieve success in the hotel and catering industry, students need a good basic arithmetical knowledge and lecturers need many examples available to supplement their lesson notes.

Get the costing wrong and the financial results can be disastrous for the hotelier and caterer. A selling price set too high will lose customers, while a selling price set too low will lose money – either way profitability will suffer.

It is recognised that hotel and catering students are not always interested in mathematical topics but, in times of inflation and price competition, a sound knowledge of costing is essential for business survival. The book is written in non-mathematical terms to present students with methods and facts that may have previously been difficult to understand.

This book is designed for students following courses leading to Hospitality and Catering GNVQ and NVQ Levels 1, 2 and 3. Those already working in the hospitality industry will benefit from the exercises graded to allow a step-by-step approach.

For this revised edition, new sections have been added on area and volume, ratio, budgeting, averages and an update on calculating for wines, spirits and liqueurs. Costs have been adjusted throughout to reflect more accurately the values currently found in the hotel and catering industry. Sample multiple choice questions like those in GNVQ end tests, are included at the back of the book.

Although not specifically required by GNVQ, the chapter on the 24 hour clock has been retained because of its importance in the hospitality industry in preventing ambiguity of timing.

In working through the book students and lecturers will find examples for discussion and it is suggested that lecturers use these questions as a basis for group topics.

BRIDGEND COLLEGE LIBRARY
CLASS No. 647.95068 GEE
COPY 00021737 PRICE £7.50
REQ. BR1002688 R27136 DATE 19/7/01

Acknowledgements

Grateful acknowledgements are due to the following who have helped in the production of this book by providing examples and technical expertise: Susan Gee (Catering Manager, Sutcliffe Catering (Southern)); George Ingham (former Deputy Head of Catering, South Fields College, Leicester); and Gerry Shurman (Course Manager GNVQ Hospitality & Catering, South Downs College, Havant).

Contents

Hospitality & Catering GNVQ Core skills, levels 1, 2 and 3

Chapter title	1.1	1.2	1.3	2.1	2.2	2.3	3.1	3.2	3.3
Addition	*	*			*			*	
Subtraction	*	*			*			*	
Multiplication	*	*			*			*	
Division	*	*			*			*	
Problems using four rules			*			*			
Area and volume		*			*	*		*	*
Cancelling	*								
Mixed numbers and improper fractions	*	*			*				
Ratio				*	*		*	*	
Percentages – expressing one amount as a % of another	*			*	*			*	
Kitchen percentages						*	*		*
Gross profit and costs				*				*	*
Depreciation			*	*				*	*
Net profit			*	*				*	*
Profit and staff meals						*	*		*
More about percentages	*	*		*	*			*	
Percentages problems			*			*	*		*
Preparing a budget						*	*		*
Averages		*	*		*	*		*	
Discount				*				*	*
Percentage puzzles				*	*				
Calculating selling price						*		*	*
Wastage						*			*
Value added tax				*	*				*
Calculating for wines, spirits and liqueurs			*	*					
Bin card	*								
The cost of sales					*	*			
GP and the cost of sales					*	*			*
The standard recipe	*								
Costing sheets	*			*					
Graphs			*			*			*
Pie charts			*			*			*
Currency conversion		*		*	*		*		

— 1 —

Addition

Without the ability to add, none of us can cost a menu, present a guest's bill, check an invoice or even work out our own wages.

How accurately can you add?

1	**2**	**3**	**4**
426	1208	3089	2464
48	875	706	38
870	99	8214	7997

5	**6**	**7**	**8**
702	2567	392	6443
8029	3829	452	27
1307	4776	8267	2877

The addition of decimals is treated in the same way. Remember that the first place behind the decimal point is the tenths column, the second place is the hundredths column, the third place is the thousandths, etc. For example:

> 14.372 is 14 whole numbers, 3 tenths, 7 hundredths and 2 thousandths.

9	**10**	**11**	**12**
4.82	18.72	175.3	401.72
20.54	4.3	19.82	248.03
0.45	32.0	311.08	36.54
34.74	77.07	12.75	74.58

13	**14**	**15**	**16**
17.27	627.34	425.38	146.27
3.05	13.2	29.72	378.72
29.77	184.17	0.37	584.47
14.23	74.23	348.27	123.97

17	**18**	**19**	**20**
£	£	£	£
87.32	443.08	67.86	124.34
0.47	85.00	29.38	25.65
25.65	27.40	17.92	308.84
1.05	18.38	74.77	0.79

21	**22**	**23**	**24**
Kilograms (kg)	kg	Litres	Litres
4.25	18.75	27.34	2.47
13.37	127.32	70.45	41.74
28.75	84.55	148.25	0.88

Sometimes it is necessary to add horizontal columns of figures. For instance, hotel receptionists often add tabular ledgers in this way.

Test your skill in working out the following:

25 4.32 + 14.74 + 30.85

26 17.05 + 48.1 + 34.56

27 81.63 + 24 + 321.28 + 50.67

28 £1.07 + £38.25 + £25.79

29 £100.38 + £324.07 + £528.39 + £35.00

30 £3.08 + £0.41 + £17.84 + £1.96

31 £0.74 + £0.32 + £0.47 + £0.89

32 £16.38 + £20.48 + £8.20 + £8.35

33 £172.39 + £75.93 + £100.49 + £45.89

34 £1,024.56 + £8.05 + £527.80 + £600.00

In some cases there is a need to give an answer to three decimal places:

1 gram (g) can be written as 0.001 kg
1 millilitre (ml) can be written as 0.001 litre
5 kg 225 g can be written as 5.225 kg

Write the following in kg:

35 7 kg 425 g
36 18 kg 350 g
37 125 kg 25 g
38 68 kg 5 g

3 litres 175 ml can be written as 3.175 litres

Write the following in litres:

39 6 litres 175 ml
40 25 litres 340 ml
41 130 litres 42 ml
42 7 litres 6 ml

43	**44**	**45**	**46**
£	£	£	£
4.127	18.34	18.205	141.255
3.038	2.278	1.005	70.185
1.245	0.045	3.128	305.295
8.005	1.36	14.00	211.384

47	**48**	**49**	**50**
kg	kg	litres	litres
40.725	21.125	17.628	65.775
128.129	39.338	50.250	20.378
0.499	8.584	49.675	71.445

— 2 —

Subtraction

1 483− 127	**2** 1432− 294	**3** 4156− 828	**4** 7243− 1738
5 £ 17.84− 3.26	**6** £ 25.62− 8.84	**7** £ 306.28− 14.49	**8** £ 1260.45− 795.63
9 kg 13.275− 8.325	**10** kg 44.184− 27.356	**11** kg 20.42− 12.65	**12** kg 125.250− 70.275
13 litres 9.25− 3.326	**14** litres 103.150− 27.326	**15** litres 45.201− 13.222	**16** litres 17.123− 0.445

17 £18.43 − £6.28

18 £36.08 − £0.36

19 £125.37 − £84.47

20 £17.36 − £8.08

21 £8.724 − £1.208

22 £18.364 − £17.842

23 13.25 kg − 8.75 kg

24 120.350 kg − 75.275 kg

25 7.46 kg − 2.72 kg

26 35.346 kg − 28.148 kg

27 81.01 litres − 9.21 litres

28 14.00 litres − 3.50 litres

29 17.125 litres − 13.250 litres

30 125.270 litres − 48.370 litres

31 Find the difference between £704.25 and £342.95

32 Find the difference between 4.275 kg and 1.791 kg

33 By how much is £56.07 greater than £27.39?

34 By how much is 25.5 litres greater than 4.125 litres?

— 3 —

Multiplication

To achieve success in this section, multiplication tables should be known.

Test your tables:

1	3×6	**2**	5×8	**3**	7×4	**4**	5×6
5	9×8	**6**	11×12	**7**	8×4	**8**	7×12
9	3×9	**10**	12×4	**11**	9×9	**12**	6×8
13	11×11	**14**	6×7	**15**	4×9	**16**	4×5
17	8×8	**18**	5×12	**19**	6×6	**20**	12×12

Now to use the tables:

21	145×6	**22**	367×7	**23**	408×8
24	125×32	**25**	423×78	**26**	374×193

In multiplying decimals, first work the sum ignoring the decimal place, e.g.

$$\begin{array}{r} 7.48\times \\ 6 \\ \hline 4488 \\ \hline \end{array}$$

Next, count the number of figures behind the decimal point in the question and place the point so that there are the same number of figures behind the point in the answer:

$$\begin{array}{r} 7.48\times \\ 6 \\ \hline 44.88 \\ \hline \end{array}$$

Here is another example:

$$\begin{array}{l} 7.48\times \\ 0.6 \\ \hline 4.488 \\ \hline \end{array}$$

NB The total number of figures behind the decimal point was three (4, 8, 6).

Here is an unusual example:

$$\begin{array}{r} 0.47\times \\ 0.12 \\ \hline 0.0564 \\ \hline \end{array}$$

Calculating the cost:

400 g @ £1.22 per kg (0.4 kg × £1.22)

$$\begin{array}{r} 1.22\times \\ 0.4 \\ \hline £0.488 \\ \hline \end{array}$$

27	17.3 × 6	**28**	42.31 × 8	**29**	17.4 × 4.3
30	£5.62 × 9	**31**	£10.35 × 7	**32**	£25.36 × 5
33	£78.42 × 63	**34**	£47.71 × 84	**35**	£30.28 × 2.5
36	£4.275 × 8	**37**	£14.128 × 13	**38**	£8.493 × 124
39	£1.25 × 4	**40**	£10.36 × 9	**41**	£2.60 × 13
42	6.275 kg × 5	**43**	1.476 kg × 12	**44**	13.75 kg × 15
45	102.5 kg × 27	**46**	14.38 kg × 42	**47**	72.125 kg × 56
48	13.5 litres × 9	**49**	2.65 litres × 21	**50**	62.5 litres × 2.5

Quick methods

17.32 × 10 = 173.2
14.25 × 100 = 1425
25.63 × 1000 = 25630

Note that the decimal point is moved one place to the right when multiplying by 10, two places when multiplying by 100, three places when multiplying by 1000 and so on.

£14.34 × 100 = £1,434.00
£3.72 × 10 = £37.20
6.75 kg × 10 = 67.5 kg
17.5 litres × 100 = 1750 litres

Try these using the quick method:

51	£4.32 × 10	**52**	£14.65 × 100	**53**	£0.14 × 1000
54	5.64 kg × 10	**55**	21.05 litres × 100	**56**	16.125 kg × 1000

— 4 —

Division

Again it is important to know the tables:

1	72 ÷ 9	**2**	144 ÷ 12	**3**	30 ÷ 6	**4**	56 ÷ 7
5	54 ÷ 9	**6**	48 ÷ 6	**7**	120 ÷ 12	**8**	45 ÷ 5
9	72 ÷ 12	**10**	27 ÷ 3	**11**	42 ÷ 6	**12**	63 ÷ 7
13	121 ÷ 11	**14**	49 ÷ 7	**15**	36 ÷ 12	**16**	35 ÷ 5
17	36 ÷ 6	**18**	81 ÷ 9	**19**	60 ÷ 12	**20**	28 ÷ 4

Using the tables:

21	824 ÷ 4	**22**	2545 ÷ 5	**23**	876 ÷ 6
24	4131 ÷ 9	**25**	3528 ÷ 7	**26**	780 ÷ 12
27	33640 ÷ 8	**28**	8041 ÷ 11	**29**	2385 ÷ 9

A common error in division is to forget the 0 in the answer to the following type of example:

$$\begin{array}{r} 1406 \\ 6\overline{)8436} \end{array}$$

Be careful in working out these questions:

30	2427 ÷ 3	**31**	545 ÷ 5	**32**	34812 ÷ 12

It is worthwhile revising the set-out of a long-division sum.

$$\begin{array}{r} 234 \\ 34\overline{)7956} \\ 68 \\ \hline 115 \\ 102 \\ \hline 136 \\ 136 \\ \hline \end{array}$$

a Having decided that 34 divides into 79 two times, put the 2 in the answer over the 9 and the 68 (2 × 34) under the 79. Subtract to find the 11 remainder.

b Keep the figures in the correct column and bring the 5 vertically down to make 115.

c Having decided that 34 divides into 115 three the 102 (3 × 34) under the 115. Subtract to find the 13 remainder.

d Keep the figures in the correct column and bring the 6 vertically down to make 136.

e Having decided that 34 divides into 136 four times, put the 4 over the 6 and the 136 under the 136. Subtract to find that there is no remainder.

33 425 ÷ 25 **34** 5550 ÷ 30 **35** 3504 ÷ 48

In decimal division the following points should be observed:

a First place the decimal point in the answer vertically above the decimal point in the question, eg

$$\begin{array}{r} . \\ 7\overline{)31.5} \end{array}$$

and then divide:

$$\begin{array}{r} 4.5 \\ 7\overline{)31.5} \end{array}$$

36 33.2 ÷ 8 **37** 16.86 ÷ 6 **38** 61.5 ÷ 3

b *Do not* divide by a decimal, eg

$$3.2\overline{)22.4}$$

Multiply both the divisor (3.2) and the dividend (22.4) by 10 and the sum now becomes

$$32\overline{)224}$$

Similarly

$$0.25\overline{)1.475}$$

becomes

$$25\overline{)147.5} \quad \text{(by multiplying by 100)}$$

39 86.1 ÷ 0.7 **40** 3.84 ÷ 0.12 **41** 0.375 ÷ 0.25

c By adding a 0 to any remainder and dividing again, a more accurate answer to a third decimal place can be obtained, eg

(i) $5\overline{)12.34}$

Answer:

$$\begin{array}{r} 2.468 \\ 5\overline{)12.340} \end{array}$$

(ii) $4\overline{)34.1}$

Answer:

$$\begin{array}{r} 8.525 \\ 4\overline{)34.100} \end{array}$$

42	63.1 ÷ 5	**43**	5.39 ÷ 4	**44**	35.6 ÷ 8

More practice in division:

45	17.12 ÷ 8	**46**	4.068 ÷ 9	**47**	37.125 ÷ 25
48	1.72 ÷ 0.4	**49**	15.48 ÷ 1.2	**50**	2.655 ÷ 0.15
51	46.21 ÷ 5	**52**	7.86 ÷ 12	**53**	28.4 ÷ 16
54	£15.24 ÷ 6	**55**	32.494 kg ÷ 7	**56**	£104.58 ÷ 42
57	£51.30 ÷ 4	**58**	15.738 litres ÷ 6	**59**	£1,136.20 ÷ 52

Sometimes an answer is required worked out to a certain number of places after the decimal point, eg

143.1 ÷ 8

Give the answer to 2 decimal places.

Answer:

$$\begin{array}{r} 17.88 \\ 8\overline{)143.10} \end{array}$$

Ignore any remainder (in this case, 6) after 2 decimal places.

60 37.45 ÷ 6 (answer to 2 decimal places)

61 £14.75 ÷ 9 (answer to 3 decimal places)

62 17.5 kg ÷ 4 (answer to 2 decimal places)

A more accurate answer can be obtained by *correcting* to a given number of decimal places, eg

Express 17.378 corrected to 2 decimal places.

Method

Look at the figure in the third decimal place and if the figure is 5 or a higher value (in this case it is 8) then add 1 to the value of the figure in the second decimal place. If the figure is lower than 5, leave the figure in the second decimal place unchanged.

17.378 corrected to 2 decimal places is 17.38

Remember: examine the figure in the second decimal place if you are correcting to 1 decimal place; examine the figure in the third decimal place if you are correcting to 2 decimal places, and so on.

Here are more examples:

1.32651 corrected to 3 decimal places is 1.327
14.183 corrected to 2 decimal places is 14.18
£405.426 to the nearest penny is £405.43.

63 14.295 corrected to 1 decimal place

64 1.8272 to 3 decimal places

65 18.4971 corrected to 3 decimal places

66 £49.128 to the nearest penny

67 21.775 kg to the nearest kg

68 143 ÷ 8 corrected to 2 decimal places

69 13.3 ÷ 4 corrected to 2 decimal places

70 £45.27 ÷ 7 corrected to 3 decimal places

Quick methods

$$421.7 \div 10 = 42.17$$
$$118.4 \div 100 = 1.184$$
$$1423 \div 1000 = 1.423$$

The decimal point is moved one place to the left when dividing by 10, two places when dividing by 100, three places when dividing by 1000 and so on.

71 14.32 ÷ 10

72 £36.42 ÷ 100

73 £11,236.00 ÷ 100

74 45 kg ÷ 10

75 410.3 litres ÷ 100

76 525 litres ÷ 1000

— 5 —

Problems using the four rules

1 Find the price of each item and total the bill:
4 kg of butter at £3.26 per kg
8 kg of sugar at £0.75 per kg
2.5 kg of flour at £0.46 per kg
100 g ground ginger at £0.70 per 50 g
3 litres of vinegar at £5.25 per 5 litres.

2 The ingredient costs in producing 2000 cups of tea are as follows:
tea – 3.75 kg at £4.00 per kg
milk – 8 litres at £0.48 per litre
sugar – 19 kg at £0.75 per kg

Find the profit made per cup if tea is sold at 45p per cup (answer to nearest penny).

3 The total food cost to produce 25 covers was £19.20. Calculate the cost per cover: **a** to 2 decimal places of £1; **b** corrected to 2 decimal places of £1.

4 The costs in producing a dinner for 50 guests were as follows:

food costs per cover	£4.22
wages	£148.50
other costs	£137.00

If the charge for the dinner was £12.50 per head, calculate the total profit made by the hotel.

5 **a** Find the cost of making 1000 cakes at £0.125 each.
b 100 cups of coffee were sold for £85.00. Find the charge per cup.

6 If 28 portions can be obtained from a turkey, how many turkeys should be ordered if 400 portions are required to be served?

7 How many 50 g portions of peas can be served from a 10 kg packet?

— 6 —

Area and Volume

The hotel industry is very much concerned with the measurement of area, especially when calculating the cost of carpeting or considering the returns per square metre of floor space. The Inland Revenue also uses floor area in determining the business rate that any catering enterprise must pay.

Example

Calculate the area of the floor shown in the diagram below.

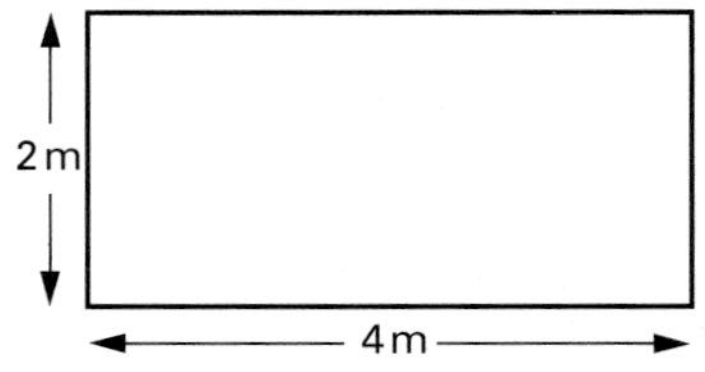

Method

The area is found by using the formula:

Area = Length × Breadth (width)
Area = 4 × 2 = 8 square metres

1 Find the area of a room 12 m in length and 5 m wide.

2 The area of a bedroom floor is 24 square metres. If the room is 6 m long, calculate its width.

3 If the measurements of a conference room were 15 m (length) × 12 m (breadth), calculate the cost of carpeting the room at £18.75 per square metre. (Assume there is no wastage.)

4 Find the area of the room shown in the diagram below.

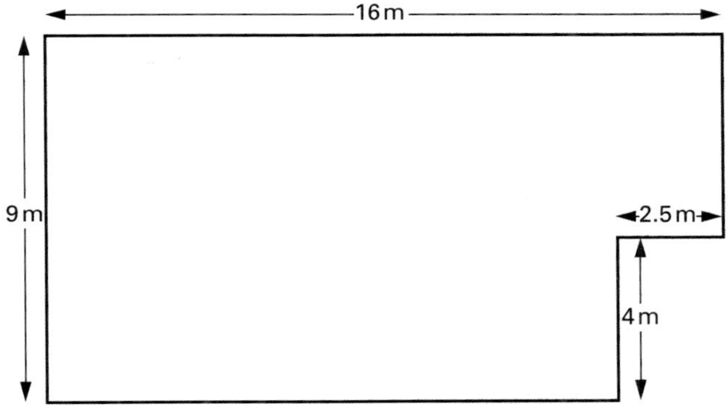

5 A hotelier needed to carpet a short stairway as represented in the sketch below.

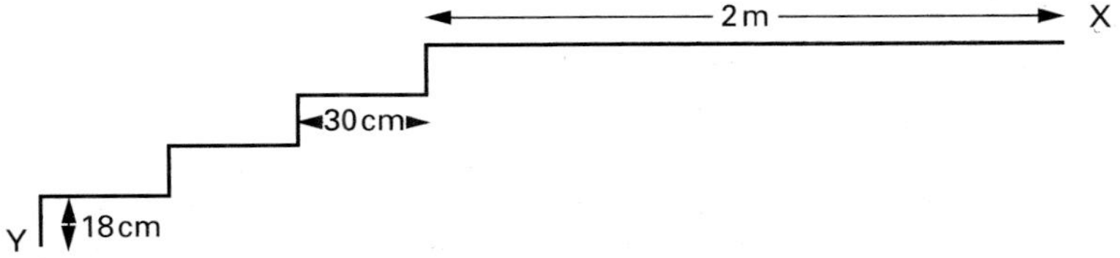

All risers are 18 cm, and except for the 2 m section, the treads measure 30 cm from rear to front.

a Find the total length of carpet required (X to Y) after allowing 0.5 m for folding.

b Calculate the cost if a 4 m wide roll of carpet is used and the price is £25 per square metre. Parts of a metre are not available.

Volume measurement is used when considering the size of air-conditioners, dehumidifiers, swimming pools and storage requirements.

The hotel and catering industry is also concerned with the volumes of drums of detergents, cooking oil and bottles of drinks. Although there is little point in being able to calculate their size, it is sensible to understand what is meant by a litre or cubic measurement.

Example

Calculate the volume of the room shown below. (Not drawn to scale.)

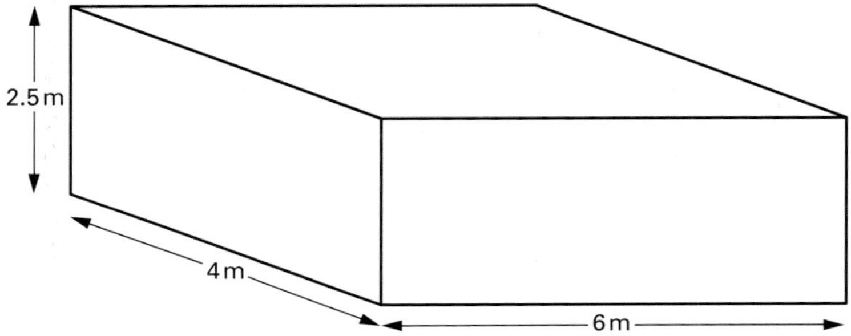

Method

The volume is found by using the formula:

Volume = Length × Breadth × Height
Volume = 6 × 4 × 2.5 = 60 cubic metres.

6 Find the volume of a room 5 m wide, 8 m long and 3 m high.

7 A room with a floor area of 48 square metres has a volume of 120 cubic metres. Calculate the height of the room.

8 **a** Would a dehumidifier, advertised to be able to cope with 150 cubic metres of air space, be suitable for a hotel bedroom and bathroom with the following dimensions:
Bedroom floor: 5.5 m × 4 m, bathroom floor: 3 m × 3 m, hallway floor: 2 m × 1.5 m, height to ceilings: 3 m?

b What is the excess or under capacity?

9 A motel owner is considering installing a swimming pool as shown in the diagram on page 13.

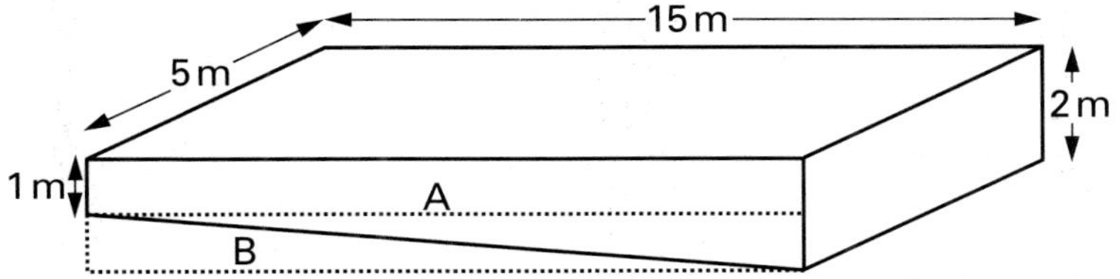

In assessing the size of a filtration plant, he must know the capacity of the pool. If one cubic metre contains 1000 litres, determine the capacity of the pool (in litres). To help you measure the side area of the pool, first calculate the area A to a depth of 1 m (as shown by the dotted line). The remaining bottom area B is bisected (halved) by the floor of the pool.

— 7 —

Cancelling

Whilst it is true to say that a correct answer in fractions and percentages can be obtained without cancelling, it is also true that cancelling at the right time makes the work simpler and quicker.

The principle of cancelling is easy to understand.

The fraction $\frac{2}{4}$ means that the 2 is being divided by 4.

By dividing the top *and* bottom lines by 2 the fraction becomes $\frac{1}{2}$:

$$\frac{2}{4} = \frac{1}{2}$$

The fraction $\frac{2}{4}$ has been divided top and bottom by 2 and becomes $\frac{1}{2}$ but the value has remained the same (two-quarters has the same value as one-half).

The secret is in finding a number that will divide *exactly* into *both* the top and bottom lines.

Examples

a Cancel $\dfrac{20}{35}$

$\dfrac{20}{35} = \dfrac{4}{7}$ (by dividing the top and bottom lines by 5).

b Cancel $\frac{125}{1000}$

$$\frac{125}{1000} = \frac{1}{8} \text{ (divide by 125).}$$

Cancel the following:

1 $\frac{40}{45}$	**2** $\frac{18}{36}$	**3** $\frac{42}{54}$	**4** $\frac{108}{144}$
5 $\frac{70}{120}$	**6** $\frac{4}{12}$	**7** $\frac{28}{35}$	**8** $\frac{6}{24}$
9 $\frac{75}{100}$	**10** $\frac{16}{64}$	**11** $\frac{17}{51}$	**12** $\frac{4000}{5000}$

— 8 —

Mixed numbers and improper fractions

Before percentages can be worked out successfully you should know how to multiply fractions and that involves mixed numbers and improper fractions.

Examples

a Change $5\frac{1}{4}$ to quarters.
(In mathematical terms the mixed number $5\frac{1}{4}$ is to be changed to an improper fraction.)

Method

In 5 whole numbers there are 20 quarters (5×4).
Therefore in $5\frac{1}{4}$ there are 21 quarters $= \frac{21}{4}$ (an improper fraction).

b Change the mixed number $3\frac{2}{5}$ to fifths.

Method

In 3 whole numbers there are 15 fifths $= \frac{15}{5}$

Therefore in $3\frac{2}{5}$ there are $\frac{17}{5}$.

1 Change $4\frac{1}{2}$ to halves

2 Change $2\frac{2}{5}$ to fifths

3 Change $7\frac{1}{4}$ to quarters

4 Change $5\frac{5}{6}$ to sixths

5 Change $10\frac{2}{3}$ to thirds

6 Change $1\frac{14}{15}$ to fifteenths

7 Change $3\frac{3}{4}$ to quarters

8 Change $2\frac{2}{7}$ to sevenths

9 Change $4\frac{3}{8}$ to eighths

10 Change $20\frac{3}{10}$ to tenths

Let us now consider changing improper fractions to mixed numbers.

Example

Change the improper fraction $\frac{20}{3}$ to a mixed number.

Method

Divide 20 by 3 = 6 whole numbers, remainder 2 thirds. Answer: $6\frac{2}{3}$.
Change to mixed numbers:

11 $\dfrac{7}{6}$

12 $\dfrac{8}{3}$

13 $\dfrac{25}{8}$

14 $\dfrac{24}{11}$

15 $\dfrac{100}{9}$

16 $\dfrac{29}{7}$

17 $\dfrac{5}{2}$

18 $\dfrac{51}{5}$

19 $\dfrac{39}{6}$ (cancel first)

20 $\dfrac{18}{8}$ (cancel first)

21 $\dfrac{100}{12}$ (cancel first)

22 $\dfrac{20}{6}$ (cancel first)

— 9 —

Multiplication of fractions

Examples

a $\dfrac{2}{3} \times \dfrac{4}{5}$

Multiply the top line, then multiply the bottom line:

$$\frac{2}{3} \times \frac{4}{5} = \frac{8}{15}$$

b $\dfrac{2}{3} \times \dfrac{6}{7}$

By cancelling, the sum is easier to work out:

$$\frac{2}{\cancel{3}_{1}} \times \frac{\cancel{6}^{2}}{7} = \frac{4}{7}$$

Remember that whatever number is divided into the top line must also be divided into the bottom line. (In the above example the division is by 3.)

c $4\frac{1}{2} \times \frac{3}{4}$

Change all mixed numbers to improper fractions before multiplying.

$$\frac{9}{2} \times \frac{3}{4} = \frac{27}{8} = 3\tfrac{3}{8}.$$

Multiplying the following:

1 $\frac{3}{5} \times \frac{4}{7}$

2 $\frac{5}{8} \times \frac{5}{6}$

3 $\frac{2}{7} \times \frac{3}{4}$

4 $\frac{6}{11} \times \frac{2}{3}$

5 $\frac{1}{2} \times 3\frac{2}{3}$

6 $2\frac{1}{2} \times \frac{3}{7}$

7 $2\frac{5}{6} \times 1\frac{1}{4}$

8 $1\frac{3}{4} \times \frac{2}{5}$

9 $6\frac{2}{3} \times 1\frac{2}{10}$

10 $5\frac{3}{4} \times 1\frac{1}{5}$

11 $1\frac{1}{2} \times 1\frac{2}{3}$

12 $2\frac{1}{2} \times 2\frac{1}{3}$

13 $2\frac{2}{3} \times 5$ (write 5 as $\frac{5}{1}$)

14 $3\frac{1}{4} \times 8$

15 $6 \times \frac{2}{3}$

16 $2\frac{3}{5} \times \frac{1}{2}$

17 Find $\frac{1}{2}$ of $2\frac{3}{4}$ ($\frac{1}{2} \times 2\frac{3}{4}$)

18 Find $\frac{3}{4}$ of $\frac{12}{17}$

19 Find $\frac{2}{3}$ of 14

20 Find $1\frac{1}{2} \times 3\frac{3}{4}$

— 10 —

Ratio

A popular recipe for making pastry involves using 2 parts flour and 1 part fat. This can be expressed as a ratio of 2 to 1 and written as 2:1.

Whatever amount of pastry is required, the ratio remains unaffected, using either pounds and ounces or kilograms and grams.

Example

A pastry mix of 360 g is made by using flour and fat in the ratio of 2:1. Find the amount needed of each ingredient.

Method

The 360 g is divided into 3 equal parts (2 parts flour + 1 part fat).

$$\begin{aligned} 360\text{ g} \div 3 &= 120\text{ g} \\ 2\text{ parts flour} &= 240\text{ g} \\ 1\text{ part fat} &= 120\text{ g} \end{aligned}$$

When added together, the separate parts must equal the total weight to be made.

$$240\text{ g} + 120\text{ g} = 360\text{ g}$$

NB Order is important. The flour was mentioned first and the 120 g must therefore be multiplied by 2; the fat as the second mentioned must be multiplied by 1.

1 If 450 g is to be split in the ratio of 7:8,
  a Into how many equal parts must the 450 g be first divided?
  b Calculate the split amounts.

2 A scone mix of flour, fat and sugar is given as being in the ratio of 8:2:2. For a mix of 2.4 kg (2400 g), calculate the amount of each ingredient.

3 The £125,000 turnover achieved by a hotel in one month was apportioned to accommodation and the restaurant in the ratio of 5:3.
  a How much was attributed to the restaurant?
  b If the labour costs usually followed the same ratio as the turnover, find the labour cost for accommodation if the restaurant labour cost was £12,000.

Care must be taken not to confuse the ratio of amounts with the parts of the whole.

Example

A squash is mixed as 1 part concentrate and 4 parts water.

a Express the proportion of concentrate to water as a ratio.

b Express the concentrate as a part or fraction of the squash mixture.

Method

a Ratio of concentrate to water = 1:4.

b Altogether there are 5 parts (1 concentrate, 4 water), there is 1 part concentrate in 5 parts of squash, or 1 in 5, ($\frac{1}{5}$).

To summarise: In mixing a squash where the ratio of concentrate to water is 1:4, there is 1 part concentrate in 5 parts squash.

4 Write the following ratios in the form 2 in ?, 1 in ?, etc
a 2:3 **b** 1:6 **c** 4:5.

5 Write the following as ratios.
a 2 in 3 **b** 4 in 9 **c** 1 in 8.

6 A barman found a successful mix for a Screwdriver cocktail was 2 parts vodka and 9 parts orange juice.
a Find the ratio of vodka to orange juice.
b What fraction of the cocktail is vodka?

Simplifying ratios

In a hotel, the snack-bar and restaurant were to share a £500,000 refurbishment in the ratio of their sales during the previous year. If the snack-bar sales amounted to £35,000 and the restaurant sales were £150,000, decide on how much money should be spent on each area.

Method

The ratio of snack-bar sales to restaurant sales is 35000:150000. That ratio can be simplified to 7:30 by dividing both numbers by 5000 as in cancelling.

7 An analysis of a hotel's records showed that during the past year, visitors staying at the hotel could be divided as follows: From the UK – 3500, from other members of the EC – 1000, from the rest of the world – 500.

To enable a proper advertising campaign to be mounted, express the visitors from the UK, the other members of the EC and the rest of the world, as a ratio in the most simplified terms.

8 A hotel management was considering the staff changing and toilet facilities. On average there are 49 male and 28 female employees. Give:

a The number of male to female staff as a ratio in the lowest terms.

b The number of female to male staff as a ratio in the lowest terms.

– 11 –

Percentages – expressing one amount as a percentage of another

Sales, costs, profit or loss, discount, occupancy – all these are expressed in percentages and it is therefore very important to be able to understand and work out percentages.

Compare these two sets of figures showing profits for a three-week period:

A. Week 1: $\frac{5}{36}$ of sales. Week 2: $\frac{4}{27}$ of sales. Week 3: $\frac{9}{80}$ of sales.
B: Week 1: 13.8% of sales. Week 2: 14.8% of sales. Week 3: 11.2% of sales.

It is much easier to compare line B to find that Week 2 had the best return on sales and yet lines A and B refer to the same weeks. It is usually more meaningful to express one amount as a percentage of another rather than as a fraction.

Examples

a Express 3p as a % of 4p

To find this comparison as a fraction, the 3p would be divided by the 4p to arrive at the answer $\frac{3}{4}$.

To express the answer as a % the fraction is multiplied by 100.

$$\frac{3}{4} \times \frac{100}{1} = 75\%$$

b Express £1.20 as a % of £4.00
(always change to pence when any one amount contains pence.)

$$\frac{120}{400} \times \frac{100}{1} = 30\%.$$

c What % of 44 is 32?

$$\frac{32}{44} \times \frac{100}{1} = 72.72\%.$$

1 Express 32 as a % of 40

2 Express 5p as a % of 25p

3 Express 40p as a % of £1.20

4 Express £5.25 as a % of £10.00

5 Express 320 g as a % of 1 kg

6 Express 50p as a % of £2.75

7 Express 4 kg as a % of 8.75 kg

8 Express 3 kg 125 g as a % of 5 kg

9 Express 12 litres as a % of 35 litres

10 Express £3,500 as a % of £7,750

11 What % of 55 is 45?

12 What % of £1.50 is £1.00?

13 What % of £0.15 is £0.04?

14 What % of 21 is 15?

15 What % of £1,000 is £175?

16 What % of 15 kg is 3.125 kg?

17 What % of £8.00 is £3.20?

18 What % of 15 litres is 5 litres 200 ml?

19 What % of £42 is £28?

20 What % of £55.50 is £20.00?

— 12 —

Kitchen percentages

For purposes of control it is useful to be able to express the costs of various groups of items used in the kitchen (main course, vegetables, dairy, etc.) as a percentage of either the total food and drink cost, or as a percentage of sales.

Example

Express each of the following costs as a percentage of the sales:

meat £30.00
vegetables £10.00
sweet £7.50

Sales £120.00

Method

Meat $\frac{30}{120} \times \frac{100}{1} = 25\%$ of sales

Vegetables $\frac{10}{120} \times \frac{100}{1} = 8.33\%$ of sales

Sweet $\frac{750}{12000} \times \frac{100}{1} = 6.25\%$ of sales.

Each group should remain fairly stable from period to period. A change in percentage should be thoroughly investigated and may be due to any of the following reasons:

a An increase in the cost of the item without a corresponding increase in the price charged.

b Poor portion control. An increase in the size of portions served would increase the percentage cost.

c Wastage through bad purchasing, poor preparation or incompetent cooking.

d Pilfering.

The increase in percentages caused by the above is due to an increase in costs needed to produce the same amount of sales.

To take another example, a meat cost of £100 required to produce sales of £500 would have risen to £150 if half of the meat had been wasted or stolen and the 20% meat to sales comparison would have risen to 30%.

1 Express each of the following costs as a percentage of the sales which were £175.00:

soup £6.00, meat £44.00, vegetables £16.00, sweets £16.00, tea and coffee £2.00.

2 The sales of a canteen for a week amounted to £2,750. Give each of the following costs as a percentage of sales:

vegetables £264, meat £924, dairy £440.

3 Give the following costs as a percentage of the total costs:

meat £1,000, vegetables £240, sweets £300, drinks £150.

4 Express each cost as a percentage of the total costs:

dairy £250, vegetables £120, meat £500.

5 Express each of the following costs as a percentage of the £220.00 sales:

milk £12.00, tea £25.20, sugar £8.00.

6 Sales in a canteen were £3,000. Express each of the following as a percentage of the sales:

meat £600, vegetables £210, sweets £160.

7 Give each of the following as a percentage of the receipts which were £29,000:

meat £6,000, vegetables £2,100, sweets £1,600.

8 In one month the comparison of meat costs to sales was 17.5%. During the next month the statistics were as follows:

sales £5,000, vegetables £350, meat £1,100, dairy £250, coffee and tea £150.

Examine the two periods and give possible reasons for any difference.

— 13 —

Gross profit and costs

In the hotel and catering industry gross profit is the difference between the price at which goods are sold and the price at which they were bought. It is sometimes referred to as 'kitchen profit'.

Example

The selling price of a dish is £1.20. The food cost of the dish is £0.44. Therefore the gross profit is 76p.

It is usual to express the gross profit as a percentage of the selling price.

Formula

$$\frac{\text{Gross profit}}{\text{Selling price}} \times \frac{100}{1}$$

eg $\frac{76}{120} \times \frac{100}{1} = \frac{190}{3} = 63.33\%$

Find the gross profit as a percentage of the selling price using the formula.

	Food cost	*Selling price*
1	10p	40p
2	£0.10	£0.15
3	£25	£75
4	3p	10p
5	£1.25	£2.00
6	£3	£5
7	£0.70	£1.50
8	£1	£2
9	£3.50	£6.50
10	£8.75	£25.00

11 The food cost of a dish is £0.35. Find the gross profit as a percentage of the selling price if the dish is sold for £0.80.

12 Goods are bought for £2.15 and sold for £3.50. Find the gross profit as a percentage of sales.

13 The ingredients cost of a cup of tea is 2p. Find the gross profit as a percentage of sales if the tea is sold for 50p per cup.

14 The total sales in a canteen during a month were £4,500 and the cost of all food and drink sold was £2,100. Find the gross profit as a percentage of sales.

15 A cake sold for 64p, cost 36p to produce. Calculate the profit as a percentage of the selling price.

16 A five-course meal was priced at £17.25. If the food and beverage cost for this meal was £6.75, what was the gross profit as a percentage of the selling price?

17 The total cost of drinks sold at an hotel bar was £2,460. If the takings amount to £5,400, calculate the gross profit as a percentage of sales.

18 A catering manager aimed to make a gross profit of 65% on sales. During a week when food and drink costs amounted to £2,050, the total sales were £5,125. By how much did the actual gross profit percentage differ from the required percentage?

19 If a catering company made sales of £165,000 in a year and costs of food and drink were £65,000, find the profit and express it as a percentage of the sales.

20 If the food cost of a dish was 38% of its selling price, find the gross profit as a percentage of the selling price.

Food cost percentage

Sometimes we need to be aware of the food or drink *cost* percentage. For instance, if a chef is required to make 60% gross profit, he may wish to check that the food cost is no higher than 40% of sales.

Example

The food cost of a dish is £0.30. The selling price of the dish is £1.05. Therefore the food cost as a percentage of sales is

$$\frac{30}{105} \times \frac{100}{1} = \frac{200}{7} = 28.57\%$$

1 The food cost of a dish is £2.50. If the selling price of the dish is £7.00, express the food cost as a percentage of the selling price.

2 The food cost of a dish priced at 75p is 25p.
a Express the food cost as a percentage of the selling price.
b Express the gross profit as a percentage of the selling price.

3 A cake was sold for £1.60. If the ingredient cost was £0.48, express this ingredient cost as a percentage of the selling price.

4 If the gross profit of a dish was 63% of the selling price, find the food cost as a percentage of the selling price.

5 A restaurant priced a bottle of wine at £11.00. If the cost of the wine to the restaurant was £5.00, express the cost as a percentage of the selling price.

— 14 —

Depreciation

As equipment gets old and wears out, it will gradually lose its value. Strong, solid items or those with few moving parts (ovens, refrigerators) may last longer than more delicate items (cash registers, computers).

This *loss of value*, very often caused by wear and tear, is known as *depreciation*. Some items may depreciate because new inventions make them redundant. In many cases hotel billing machines have been replaced by computers.

One simple method of working out depreciation is shown by the following example:

Example

An oven is estimated to be usable for 10 years and is purchased for £2,000. Calculate its value after 3 years (assume it loses value equally each year and there is no resale value after the 10 years).

10 years' loss is £2,000
1 year's depreciation is £200
3 years' depreciation is £600

Therefore the value after 3 years is £1,400.

1 A cash register costing £2,500 is reckoned to have a working life of five years. Calculate its value at the end of two years.

2 The tables and chairs in a restaurant had to be replaced after eight years. If the original cost was £10,000, what was the average depreciation per year?

3 A car was purchased for £14,000. If the Inland Revenue agrees to the revaluing of the car after 12 months to £10,500, express the depreciation as a percentage of the original price.

4 A manager allows for the depreciation of a dishwasher at the rate of £150 per year for twelve years. Calculate the price paid for the machine.

5 A refrigerator bought in March 1987 for £350 was estimated to be worth £150 in March 1989. Calculate the percentage loss by depreciation over the two years.

6 The following purchases were made on 1 January:

oven £3,000, washing machine £500, tables and chairs £8,000.

If each item is estimated to have a life of eight years, calculate the total depreciation that must be allowed after one year.

7 A caterer purchased an oven for £2,000. He expected the oven to have a working life of ten years and set aside £200 each year for depreciation. Would he have sufficient funds saved to replace the oven at the end of its estimated working life? (For discussion.)

— 15 —

Net profit

In finding the gross profit, only the materials cost (food and drink) has been taken into account, but there are two other costs that must be considered – labour and overheads.

Labour costs include wages, staff meals, national insurance, staff accommodation and training.

Overheads include business rates, rent, gas and electricity, telephone, stationery, insurance, advertising, repairs and depreciation.

Net profit is therefore the difference between the price at which goods are sold and the *total costs* (materials, labour, overheads).

These total costs are known as the *elements of cost.*

Example

The food cost of producing a dinner for The Evergreen Club was £37.50. The labour costs were reckoned at £23.25 and overheads estimated at £18.00. If The Evergreen Club was charged £93.75 for the dinner, calculate the net profit as a percentage of sales.

Food cost	£37.50
Labour	£23.25
Overheads	£18.00
Total costs	£78.75

Sales	£93.75
Total costs	£78.75
Net profit	£15.00

The net profit (£15.00) is usually expressed as a percentage of sales.

$$\frac{1500}{9375} \times \frac{100}{1} = 16\%.$$

1 Calculate the net profit as a percentage of sales from the following information:
food cost £3.20, labour costs £3.00, overheads £2.75, sales £10.00.

2 The following figures were extracted from the books of The Blue Moon Restaurant. Food cost £200, labour and overheads £295, sales £550. Find as a percentage of sales: **a** gross profit; **b** net profit.

3 Find the percentage net profit on sales from the following statistics:

food cost £800, labour £750, rent and rates £300, telephone £120, stationery £80, power £200, sales £2,500.

4 A catering establishment made a gross profit of £1,000. If labour costs were £450 and overheads £425, find the net profit.

5 If the gross profit was 60% of sales and the net profit was 10% of sales, calculate: **a** the food cost as a percentage of sales; **b** the total costs as a percentage of sales.

6 If the total cost to a hotel of a dinner for 50 guests was £585 and the guests were charged £13.50 per head, find: **a** the net profit per cover; **b** the net profit as a percentage of sales.

7 The returns for a school meals service were as follows:
total receipts £10,000, total costs £21,000.
Calculate the net figure as a percentage of receipts.

8 **a** Is it possible for a function to show a gross profit but a net loss?

b Is it possible for a function to show a gross loss but a net profit?

9 A caterer quoted £1,200 as the price for a buffet at a wedding with 80 guests. If he allowed £6.20 per head for the cost of food and beverages, £316 for labour costs and £190 for overheads, calculate the net profit he expected as a percentage of the quote.

10 The total sales of a restaurant over a year amounted to £338,000. The cost of food and drink was £136,000 and labour, rent, rates, power and other costs totalled £170,000. What was the net profit as a percentage of the sales?

11 For a period of one week the returns of catering establishment *A* were: sales £12,500, food cost £6,000, labour costs £3,000, overheads £2,400.
Over the same period the returns for catering establishment *B* were: sales £10,000, food cost £3,950, labour costs £2,550, overheads £2,500.

a Calculate

(i) the net profit of *A*
(ii) the net profit of *A* as a percentage of sales
(iii) the net profit of *B*
(iv) the net profit of *B* as a percentage of sales.

b Which establishment do you think was the more successful? (For discussion.)

c If the owners of *A* and the owners of *B* had each invested £360,000 in their businesses, which owners received the better percentage returns on their money?

d Should the net profit percentage of sales be the final consideration in assessing the success of a business? (For discussion.)

— 16 —

Profit and staff meals

In the previous section, staff meals were shown as a labour cost. Why is this so? Consider the following details extracted from the books of a restaurant:

> food cost £600, wages £400, rates £150, power £100, advertising £100, telephone £80, staff meals £50, sales £1,750.

If staff meals are counted as part of the overall food cost, the profits would be calculated as follows:

Sales	£1,750	
Food cost	£ 650	(£600 + £50)
Gross profit	£1,100	= 62.85% of sales
Gross profit	£1,100	−
Wages & overheads	£ 830	
Net profit	£ 270	= 15.42% of sales.

If staff meals are included as part of the labour costs, the profits would be calculated as follows:

Sales	£1,750	
Food cost	£ 600	
Gross profit	£1,150	= 65.71% of sales
Gross profit	£1,150	−
Labour & overheads	£ 880	
Net profit	£ 270	= 15.42% of sales.

Including the cost of staff meals with the food cost has the effect of reducing the gross profit and this is unfair on the chef trying to achieve a required gross profit percentage. It is usual to allow the chef an agreed amount to cater for staff.

Note that the net profit is not affected whichever method is used because that is a final figure with *all* costs subtracted.

1 The following details are taken from the Five Ways Restaurant: food cost £1,000, labour costs £810, overheads £775, sales £3,000.

a Calculate: (i) the gross profit as a percentage of sales; (ii) the labour costs as a percentage of sales; (iii) the net profit as a percentage of sales.

Later it was discovered that the £100 cost of staff meals had in error been included in the food cost and not in the labour costs.

b Using the corrected figures calculate: (i) the gross profit as a percentage of sales; (ii) the labour costs as a percentage of sales; (iii) the net profit as a percentage of sales.

2 Find the gross profit from the following information: food consumed by customers £250, food consumed by staff £50, drink consumed by customers £190, total sales £1,500.

3 The week's returns prepared by a manager of a café showed a gross profit of £10,500. By mistake, staff meals amounting to £300 had been included in the general food cost. Find the true gross profit.

4 A manager transferred the staff meals cost of £280 from the food cost to the labour costs. What effect would that have on the net profit figure of £2,080?

— 17 —

More about percentages

So far we have been concerned with expressing one amount as a percentage of another but it is also useful to be able to find a given percentage of an amount, eg find 3% of £25.50.

1% is one hundredth ($\frac{1}{100}$) and to find one hundredth of an amount we divide it by 100. There are two methods of working out this type of sum and both involve dividing it by 100 to find 1% and then multiplying to find the required percentage.

Example

Find 3% of £25.50

Method 1

$$\frac{3 \times 25.50}{100} = \frac{76.50}{100} = £0.765.$$

Method 2

1% of £25.50 = £0.255 (division by 100), therefore 3% = £0.765 (multiplication of decimals).

Find 1% of the following:

1	£570	**2**	£1,425	**3**	£306
4	455 kg	**5**	25 litres	**6**	£126.50

7	Find 2% of £675	**8**	Find 6% of £1,034
9	Find 20% of £2,450	**10**	Find 8% of 175 kg
11	Find 15% of 250 litres	**12**	Find 4% of 500 kg
13	Find 35% of £4,000	**14**	Find 2% of £5.75
15	Find 25% of £400	**16**	Find 10% of 140 kg
17	Find 20% of £25,000	**18**	Find 3% of £18.50
19	Find 5% of 75 kg	**20**	Find 40% of 80 litres
21	Find 16% of 5000 customers	**22**	Find 15% of 120 eggs

— 18 —

Percentage problems

1 55% of hospital patients were on special diets. If on average there are 800 patients in a hospital, calculate the number on a diet.

2 A hotel manager required his chef to make a gross profit of 60% on sales. Calculate the gross profit the manager expected on sales of £1,270.

3 A restaurant charged £9.00 plus a service charge for a meal. Find the total charged for a group of two couples if the service charge was 12%.

4 A restaurant averaged 550 customers per week before raising its prices, which resulted in a drop of 4% of customers. How many customers are now served per week?

5 A caterer's sales amounted to £12,500. Find the overheads if the caterer estimated these to be 22% of sales.

6 A wine merchant advised all customers that prices would be increased by 6%. Find the new price of a bottle of wine previously sold for £5.60. (Give your answer to the nearest penny.)

7 A caterer allowed 12% for depreciation per year on the value of his large-scale equipment. If he purchased a deep freeze for £1,250, find the estimated value after 12 months.

8 The electricity board announced a $2\frac{1}{2}$% increase in the price of electricity. If over the previous 12 months a hotelier's electricity bill was £2,750, what could he expect to pay over the next 12 months, assuming that his electricity consumption stays constant?

9 A caterer always allowed 30% of sales as a charge to labour. Sales from a function brought in £1,100 and he found that the labour costs were £305. Find the difference between his estimated labour costs and the actual labour costs.

10 The Inland Revenue allowed a caterer to reduce (depreciate) the value of his car by 25% per year for tax purposes. Calculate the value after one year of a car purchased for £13,500.

11 If 55% was the percentage gross profit expected on the sales of drinks, calculate the estimated gross profit on drink-sales of £1,270.

12 The food cost to a hotel for a period of a week was £2,560. If the hotelier estimated that the hotel staff meals accounted for 22% of the food cost, what was the cost of the food consumed by the guests?

13 A chef reckoned that in frying fish there was an absorption of 12% of cooking oil. How much was remaining if the chef started with 5 litres of oil?

— 19 —

Preparing a budget

Weather forecasting and financial budgeting have a lot in common – a little bit of luck, a great deal of guesswork backed up with facts, experience and a sense of history are all combined to try and predict the future.

1 Look back over the past year and list the differences between your *expectations* in terms of income and expenditure and your *actual* income and expenditure. Try to account for the difference (eg increase/decrease in income, transport costs, meals, taxes, gas and electricity).

All business owners should regularly think about how future trading conditions will affect their business. Points to consider might include:

> customer affluence (employment prospects), interest rates, pay settlements, price fluctuations, rent/rates increases, competition, trends (eating habits – weight watchers, food scares).

There will be no certainty in the overall predictions, but a considered approach is better than a 'wait and see' attitude.

This crystal gazing may cause the owner to change his or her pricing policy, reduce or increase a bank overdraft, cut the number of staff, employ more staff, change suppliers, move premises – or sell up and retire.

2 Produce your own budget for the next 12 months based on money you expect to receive (eg earnings, grants, pocket money, gifts) and your projected outgoings (eg accommodation, meals, travel, clothes, entertainment, holidays, subscriptions). Balance your income and expenditure each month and carry the balance forward to the next month. Try to estimate increases and decreases, using your experience.

3 The income and expenditure of the High Falls restaurant in June were as follows:

> Food sales £35,000, drink sales £6,500, food costs £14,000, drink costs £2,300, labour full-time costs £7,800, labour part-time costs £3,200, rent/rates £5,000, telephone £200, power £1,500, advertising £850, insurance £750, miscellaneous £1,050.

a Copy the proforma set out on page 33 and enter the above details in the June column to find the net profit.

	June	July
Income		
Food		
Drink		
Total (X)		
Expenditure		
Food		
Drink		
Labour:		
F/T		
P/T		
Rates/Rent		
Telephone		
Power		
Advertising		
Insurance		
Miscellaneous		
Total (Y)		
Net Profit (X-Y)		

b The estimates for July, based on the June figures were: Food sales – increase of 10%, drink sales – increase of 8%, food costs – increase of 10%, drink costs – increase of 8%, labour (full-time) – extra overtime of £250, labour (part-time) – increase of £500, rates/rent – no change, telephone – increase of £25, power – increase of 5%, advertising – increase of £100, insurance – no change, miscellaneous – an extra £550.

Enter the estimations in the July column to find the projected net profit.

c Later the hotelier considered even more advertising and calculated that if he spent an additional £100, the sales and costs for food and drink could increase by 1.5%.

(i) Ignoring other costs, should he take more advertising space?
(ii) Find the new estimated net profit for July (to nearest £10).

4 In the previous summer during the period June, July and August, a hotel had total sales of £1,250,000 offset by total costs of £1,120,000. On preparing the next year's budget, the hotelier had estimated an increase in sales of 8% and an increase in costs of 5%. Poor weather during the summer resulted in actual sales of £1,220,750 and costs of £1,103,200.

a Calculate for the 3 month period the difference between the estimated profit and the actual profit.

b Compare the increases/decreases in sales and costs and give a reason for any proportional difference (discuss).

— 20 —

Averages – mean, median and mode

The art of reading and using statistics is in the ability to extract the particular information required. This chapter deals with the understanding and selection of 'average' values.

Example

On carrying out a survey, the owner of a snack-bar found that in one week 960 customers spent a total of £2,400. Find the average amount spent by each customer.

Method

Divide the amount spent by the number of customers.

£2,400 ÷ 960 = £2.50

This is the most common use of the term 'average' and it is known as the *mean*, or *arithmetic mean*. If we assumed each customer spent exactly the same amount of money, the answer would have been the same.

1 Find the mean average amount spent by the following customers.

a Sales £120, customers 40.

b Sales £2,050, customers 100.

c Sales £392.50, customers 50.

2 If the mean spend by 20 customers was £8, calculate the total sales.

Sometimes it is useful to be able to find the middle or *median* value. In the example given above, it was shown that the mean amount spent was £2.50, but it could be that no customer actually spent that amount. Consider the statistics below.

Example

Nine customers spent the following: A £2, B £12, C £4, D £2, E £14, F £4, G £9, H £4, I £3.

The arithmetic mean is £54 ÷ 9 = £6 (*NB* not one customer spent £6).

Find the median amount.

Method

By arranging the sums of money in ascending order, the medium average is obtained by finding the middle value as shown by the underlined amount below:

£2, £2, £3, £4, <u>£4</u>, £4, £9, £12, £14.

The median is £4 and the amounts spent are spread equally above and below that amount.

The median shows that as many customers are likely to spend more than £4 as less than £4, and any distortion due to an unusually high or unusually low spending customer is evened out.

If there are an even number of amounts, eg £2, £4, £8, £12, then the median is the arithmetic mean of the middle two amounts:

(£4 + £8) ÷ 2 = £6

3 Find **a** the mean **b** the median of the following:

£7, £19, £8, £6, £3, £7, £6.

4 An analysis of receipts showed that the following orders were taken at lunch time:

3 @ £7.50, 4 @ £6.00, 4 @ £12.00, 7 @ £8.50, 8 @ £4.25, 10 @ £9.00

Find the median average amount taken.

5 The number of guests in residence at a hotel during one week were as follows:

Mon 30, Tues 25, Wed 42, Thur 48, Fri 10, Sat 15, Sun 5.

Calculate

a the average (mean) number of guests staying per night.
b the median of the number of guests per night.

6 Find the median value of £200, £600, £1,000, £200, £800, £400.

Another useful value is the *mode*. This is used when the most frequent number or amount is required.

Example

Over a two week period a hotel recorded the following occupancy levels:

Mon 60%, Tues 55%, Wed 80%, Thurs 75%, Fri 30%, Sat 90%, Sun 10%, Mon 55%, Tues 55%, Wed 55%, Thurs 80%, Fri 30%, Sat 75%, Sun 15%.

Find the most common (mode) occupancy.

Method

List the frequency of each percentage as below.

%	frequency	%	frequency
10	1	55	4
15	1	60	1
30	2	80	1
		90	1

By studying the frequency chart, it can be found that the most common occupancy is 55% which occurs on 4 occasions. Therefore the mode average is 55%. This could be useful when deciding on the number of staff required – it could act as a starting point when deciding on manning levels.

7 A new landlord of a pub was attempting to establish staffing levels. He had the following information, which shows the number of customers (to the nearest 10) over the previous four week period.

Number of evenings	Number of customers
4	20
6	30
3	40
2	50
10	60
3	70

Find the modal average of the number of customers.

8 You are provided with limited data which shows that 150 customers spent £450 in total.

a Find the average spend per customer.
b Say whether your answer gives the mean, median, or mode.

9 A county meals service kept details of staff physical proportions for the ordering and stocking of uniforms. Discuss which of the 'averages' gives the best information to determine the sizes of uniforms to order.

— 21 —

Discount

Giving discount – which means reducing the price of an article because the customer buys in bulk (trade discount), or pays the bill promptly (cash discount) – is used much less now due to a number of factors. Price competition between suppliers means that prices differ without the action of discount. Drivers are aware of differences in the price of petrol. Customers can, and do, shop around to find the best price. The best price may not always be the lowest price when quality is considered. Many suppliers rely on huge volumes of trade to maintain their profitability, and in many cases profit margins are so low that giving discount cannot be afforded.

Cash discount, which is offered for prompt payment, is almost non-existent now in the catering industry although a few suppliers may offer around 1% discount for quick payment. In certain industries (but not the food industry) it is *advantageous* for suppliers to sell on credit because finance houses (moneylenders) give the suppliers a share of the interest charged to their customers.

Prices these days are often negotiable, usually depending upon the amount of goods a customer purchases, and are not likely to be quoted at a discount although it operates in a similar way to trade discount.

Here are a few discount questions.

1 A restaurant owner buys goods amounting to £300 per month (at normal prices). Find the total money saved over 12 months if the rate of discount he received was 1%.

2 A dishwasher was priced by supplier *A* at £2,056. The same model dishwasher was offered by supplier *B* at £2,150 less 5% discount. Which supplier was the cheaper and by how much?

3 An advertisement by a supplier of cash registers read as follows, 'All manufacturers' recommended prices slashed by 20%.' Find the asking price for a cash register priced by the manufacturer at £1,880.

4 The central purchasing department of a town hall was given a 15% discount of all cleaning materials. Find the cost to the Schools' Meals Service of a drum of washing-up detergent if the usual advertised price was £35 per drum.

5 A firm offered $1\frac{1}{2}$% discount for prompt payment of bills and a customer could just afford to pay his bill but also needed money to buy extra equipment from another supplier. If the customer borrowed money from a bank, he would be charged 12% interest. Do you think the customer would:

a pay the firm the money owed, thereby receiving the cash discount, and borrow the money required for the equipment from a bank?
OR

b not pay the firm, so losing the cash discount, and buy the equipment without having to borrow from the bank? (For discussion.)

In question 3, if 20% was deducted from the original price then 80% will be left to pay. Calculate the answer by finding 80% of £1,880. Use this method to find the answer to question 4. You may prefer this method, especially if you are using a calculator.

— 22 —
Percentage puzzles

Examples

a If 6p is 2% of an amount, what is 1%?

Method

6p = 2%

then $\frac{6}{2}$ = 1% (this is a very important mathematical step to understand)

therefore 3p = 1%.

b If £24 is 8% of an amount, find 1%.

Method

If 24 $= 8\%$

then $\frac{24}{8} = 1\%$

$= £3.$

1 If £50 = 25%, find 1%.

2 If £65 = 5%, find 1%.

3 If 36 kg = 24%, find 1%.

4 If 40 litres = 8%, find 1%.

5 If £250 = 16%, find 1%.

Examples

c 6p is 2% of an amount, find 15%.

Method

If 6p $= 2\%$

then $\frac{6}{2} = 1\%$

therefore $\frac{6}{2} \times \frac{15}{1} = 15\%$

$= 45\text{p}.$

d If £0.70 = 20% find 32%.

Method

$\frac{70}{20} = 1\%$

$\frac{70}{20} \times \frac{32}{1} = 32\%$

$= £1.12.$

e If 30 is 40% of a certain number, what is the number (100%)?

Method

$\frac{30}{40} = 1\%$

$\frac{30}{40} \times \frac{100}{1} = 100\%$

$= 75$ (the number required).

6 If 21 is 35% of a number, what is the number?

7 If £0.14 is 20% of an amount, find 45%.

8 If 9 kg is 12% of an amount, find 80%.

9 If £33 is 11%, find 85%.

10 If 3 litres is 15%, find 100%.

11 If 81 kg is 18% of an amount, find 20%.

12 15% of a delivery of eggs were cracked. If 18 eggs were cracked, how many were delivered?

13 If 40% of the selling price of a dish was food cost, find the selling price if the food cost was £1.20.

14 If 15% was absorbed but 850 ml remained, calculate the original amount (100%).

15 Sixteen female students represented 80% of a class. How many students were in the class altogether?

16 A caterer estimated that 20% of meat was wasted in preparation. If 3 kg were wasted how many kilograms were delivered?

17 A restaurateur made £1,000 net profit, which was 8% of sales. Calculate the sales.

18 A hotel chain raised the price of all double rooms by 5% resulting in an increase of £2.50. Find the original price.

19 The price of a meal included £1.05 for VAT at 17.5%. What amount of money was retained by the restaurateur?

20 A chef requested a pay rise of 10% but he was given 6% and that raised his gross weekly pay by £10.80. Calculate the increase he requested.

— 23 —

Calculating the selling price

A bad pricing policy can quickly ruin a business. Overpricing will result in a loss of custom and underpricing can result in money being lost each time a dish is sold. A particular dish may be very popular because it is cheap (and underpriced), and so the more dishes sold the greater will be the loss.

One method of pricing a dish is to work on a fixed percentage of sales determined by experience.

A formula to remember:

$$\textit{cost + profit = selling price (100\%)}$$

NB The selling price is always 100%.

Examples

a Find the selling price to achieve a gross profit of 60% on the selling price if the food cost is 36p.

Method

Cost + profit (60%) = selling price (100%)

therefore the cost = 40% (100% − 60%)

or 36p = 40%

thus $\frac{36}{40} = 1\%$

$$\frac{36}{40} \times \frac{100}{1} = 100\% \text{ (selling price)}$$
$$= 90\text{p}$$

The selling price must be 90p.

b Find the sales necessary to achieve a net profit of 10% on sales if the total costs are £19.80.

Method

If the profit is 10%, then the costs are 90%
therefore £19.80 (costs) = 90%

$$\frac{19.80}{90} \times \frac{100}{1} = 100\% \text{ (selling price)}$$
$$= £22.00.$$

1 Find the selling price necessary to achieve a gross profit of 65% on the selling price if the food cost of a dish is £0.63.

2 A dish was costed out at £2.00. What should be charged to achieve 60% gross profit on the selling price?

3 If the total costs for a buffet were £96.00, what should be charged to give a net profit of 12% on sales? (Answer to the nearest £.)

4 The following figures were calculated for the Tigers Rugby Club's annual dinner: food cost £750, labour and overheads £1,680. What must be charged to achieve a net profit of 10% on sales?

5 The food cost of a dish was calculated as £1.35. What should be charged to achieve a net profit of 10% on sales?

6 In quoting for a luncheon a caterer estimated the costs as follows: food £110, labour £78, overheads £83. If the caterer allowed for a net profit of 10% on sales calculate the price quoted to the nearest £.

7 **a** Find the selling price of the following dishes in order to achieve a gross profit of $66\frac{2}{3}$% on the selling price: food cost (i) 25p, (ii) 32p, (iii) £2.50.

b Compare the selling price with the food cost for each dish. Can you discover a simple method of finding the answer when the gross profit required is $66\frac{2}{3}$% of the selling price?

8 A hotelier wished to make 55% gross profit on sales for all drinks served at the bar. What must be charged for a bottle that cost the hotelier £3.60?

9 An industrial catering manageress was required to make 50% gross profit on sales. Find the charge made per meal if the average food cost of a meal was £1.75.

10 The ingredient cost for a cup of tea was 1.5p. Calculate the charge per cup if 95% gross profit on the sales was made.

11 A chef was required to make 60% gross profit on sales. He had priced a dish at £6.00 but on costing the dish again he found the food cost had risen to £2.80. By how much should he increase the price to achieve the required gross profit?

12 Give the selling price to achieve a gross profit of $66\frac{2}{3}$% on sales if the ingredient cost was £1.95.

13 The total costs of a dinner for 100 guests were £1,500. What should be the charge per head in order to receive a net profit of 15% on sales? (Answer to nearest 5p.)

14 Discuss this statement, 'One fixed rate of percentage gross profit for every dish sold may not always be the best policy.'

15 Find the selling price of a dish costing 95p to produce, if a gross profit of 65% on the selling price was obtained. (Answer to nearest 5p.)

16 The total costs involved in catering for a disco were estimated at £350. If the caterer required a net profit of 10% on sales, what should be charged to cater for this event? (Answer to nearest £.)

17 The £500 sales for a week showed a gross profit of 60% on sales. What should the sales have been in order to have made a gross profit of 65% on sales?

18 An industrial contract caterer required 12% net profit on sales. If the total costs per meal averaged £2.86, what subsidy per meal should be requested from the client if the price to the workers must be restricted to £2.25 per meal?

19 A canteen manageress aimed to make a gross profit of 60% on sales. The figures for the week were: food cost £253.40, sales £700.00.

a What was the actual gross profit achieved as a percentage of sales?

b By how much did the estimated gross profit differ from the actual gross profit?

20 What are the advantages and disadvantages of fixing selling prices *after* considering competitors' prices? (For discussion.)

— 24 —

Wastage

Wastage occurs during preparation and cooking; it can be due to poor buying or lack of culinary skills. It is sensible to be able to calculate how much wastage occurs and to be able to order accordingly.

Example

A caterer took delivery of 20 kg of meat. After wastage in preparation and cooking only 14 kg of meat was served. What percentage of the original delivery was wasted?

Method

Delivery	20 kg
Served	14 kg
Wasted	6 kg

Percentage of delivery wasted

$$= \frac{6}{20} \times \frac{100}{1} = 30\%.$$

1 Out of a delivery of 30 kg of meat there was a wastage of 12 kg. Calculate the percentage of the delivery that was wasted.

2 A caterer ordered and received 35 kg of meat. The meat produced 84 portions of 125 g. What percentage of the original order was wasted?

Although it is useful to be able to find the percentage wasted, it is much more important to be able to calculate the correct amount to order *after* allowing for wastage.

Example

A caterer required to serve 14 kg of meat. By experience the caterer estimates that 30% of the meat would be wasted during the preparation and cooking. How much meat should the caterer order?

Method

Let amount of meat ordered	= 100%
Amount wasted	= 30% (of order)
Therefore meat to be served	= 70% (of order)
But meat to be served	= 14 kg
therefore 14 kg	= 70% (of order)
therefore 100% $= \frac{14}{70} \times \frac{100}{1}$	= 20 kg
Amount of meat to be ordered	= 20 kg.

In the following questions calculate all answers to the nearest kg.

3 A chef estimated that he would require 13 kg of meat after wastage. If he allowed 35% for wastage, find the amount of meat the chef should order.

4 A caterer needed to serve 25 kg of meat. Calculate the amount of meat to be ordered if 40% was allowed for wastage.

5 Find the weight of fish to be ordered if a chef required 10 kg at the table and he estimated a wastage rate of 25% of delivery.

6 One hundred 120 g portions of meat were required. Allowing 45% for wastage, how much meat should be ordered?

7 A caterer required to serve 20 kg of meat. If he allowed 40% for wastage in preparation and cooking, calculate the total cost to the caterer if the meat was priced at £6 per kg.

8 Allowing 38% for wastage, calculate the amount of meat to be ordered if 35 kg was required to be served.

9 By using butcher *A* a wastage of 25% would need to be allowed for but by using butcher *B* the wastage would average 38%. If 25.5 kg was required to be served and *A* charged £4 per kg and

B charged £3.75 per kg, which butcher was the cheaper overall and by how much?

10 What factors must be taken into account in deciding on the best supplier? (For discussion.)

— 25 —

Value Added Tax

Like all taxes, VAT is a means of raising money for public services. Although the Government can raise or lower the rate, it is controlled to some extent by the rules of the European Community (EC).

VAT is a customer tax, ie, the cost of the tax is added to a customer's bill and is not paid by a hotel or catering enterprise providing they are registered for VAT purposes (which depends on their turnover).

A registered business can charge and reclaim VAT – look out for the VAT registration number on a bill. All money collected for this tax is sent to HM Customs & Excise.

Example

A caterer charges £20.00 + VAT for a meal. If the rate of VAT is 17.5%, calculate the total price charged.

Method

Money required by the caterer	= £20.00
VAT @ 17.5%	= £ 3.50
Price paid by the customer	= £23.50

The total price paid by the customer could also be found by multiplying £20.00 by 117.5% (or 1.175 as a decimal), especially if using a calculator or programming a computer.
NB The £3.50 is sent to Customs & Excise.

1 A restaurant charges £12.00 + VAT @ 17.5% for a bottle of wine. Calculate the total price paid by the customer for this bottle of wine.

2 The basic price of a double room at a hotel was £80.00. If VAT @ 17.5% was added to the basic price, find the additional cost charged to the guests.

3 A caterer required 10% net profit on a buffet costing £180 to produce. Calculate the total price charged by the caterer if the rate of VAT was 17.5%.

4 A caterer required £14.00 + VAT for a meal for one person. Find the total price paid by a customer paying for two meals if the rate of VAT was:

a 17.5%
b 20%
c 18%.

Deducting VAT

Example

A caterer prices a dinner for 20 guests at £188 (inclusive of VAT at 17.5%).

Calculate:
a the amount retained by the caterer.
b the amount sent to Customs & Excise.

Method

$$\begin{aligned} \text{The price inclusive of VAT} &= \text{basic price} \times 1.175 \\ £188 &= \text{basic price} \times 1.175 \\ \text{basic price} &= £188 \div 1.175 \\ &= £160 \end{aligned}$$

a amount retained by caterer = £160
b amount sent to Customs & Excise = £28

The table below can be used to find the amount retained by an establishment.

VAT rate	Divide total selling price by
8%	1.08
17.5%	1.175
18%	1.18
20%	1.2
22%	1.22

5 A menu showed the price of a meal at £9.40 (inclusive of VAT @ 17.5%). Find the amount of money that will be retained by the catering establishment.

6 A husband and wife were presented with a bill for £141.00 for a special weekend offer at a hotel. Calculate the amount that would be sent later to Customs & Excise if the rate of VAT was 17.5%.

7 A bottle of red wine was priced by a restaurateur at £15.00. If VAT had been added at 20%, find the amount retained by the restaurateur.

8 The total takings in a restaurant on one evening was £1,410. Assuming all the takings were liable for VAT at a rate of 17.5%, how much money would be retained by the restaurant?

— 26 —

Calculating for wines, spirits and liqueurs

Useful information

10 millilitres (ml) = 1 centilitre (cl)
100 centilitres = 1 litre
1 litre = 1.8 pints (approximately)

1 Using the above information calculate:
 a how many millilitres are equal to 1 litre?
 b how many centilitres are equal to 300 millilitres?

Example

How many times can a 25 ml measure be filled from a 2 litre container of liquid?

Method

$$2 \text{ litres} = 2000 \text{ ml}$$
$$2000 \div 25 = 80$$

Therefore 80 measures can be filled.

The law

An establishment can choose to sell spirits either by a 25 ml measure or a 35 ml measure. Whichever size of measure is chosen, the Weights & Measures Act 1985 dictates that a notice must be displayed showing the size of measure for gin, rum, whisky and vodka.

2 If the term 'double measure' refers to two measures and 'triple measure' refers to three measures, find how many ml are contained in

  a a double 25 ml measure
  b a triple 35 ml measure.

3 A publican elected to serve spirits in measures of 25 ml.

  a How many single measures can be obtained from a 75 cl bottle of vodka?
  b How many double measures can be dispensed from a 1.5 litre bottle of scotch?
  c How many double measures can be obtained from a half litre of cherry brandy?

Glasses of wine must be sold in measures of 125 ml or 175 ml or multiples of these amounts; eg:

$$2 \times 125 \text{ ml} = 250 \text{ ml}.$$

4 Using a 175 ml measure, how many glasses of wine can be filled from a 70 cl bottle of Merlot?

5 Find the number of 75 cl bottles of wine required to serve 36 glasses using the 125 ml measure.

6 Approximately how many pints of beer are equal (in capacity) to a pack of 20 litre cans of lager?

7 The Mountain View restaurant uses a 25 ml measure for dispensing spirits but the Railway Inn uses a 35 ml measure. Calculate which establishment has the highest return and by how much, on a 70 cl bottle of brandy if both establishments charge £2.25 per single measure.

8 A 50 ml measure of sherry was allowed per guest at a wedding reception catering for 150 people. Using this measure, find the total price that should be charged before the addition of VAT to provide sufficient drinks if a 75 cl bottle of sherry cost the caterer £3.00, and he requires a profit of 55% on the sales. (Give your answer to the nearest £1.)

9 The organiser of a reception for 60 guests allowed two glasses of wine per person. On past experience she assumed 20% of the guests would prefer to drink fruit juice and 75% of the wine drinkers would choose the white wine. Using a measure of 125 ml per glass, how many 75 cl bottles of **a** white wine **b** red wine, did she assume would be required?

10 How many 35 ml measures can be obtained from a litre of spirit?

11 A 75 cl bottle of Chardonnay cost a restaurateur £4.80. Using a measure of 125 ml as his standard, find the price per glass the

restaurateur should charge in order to achieve a gross profit of 60% on the selling price, if the rate of VAT is 17.5%.

12 Records show that forty 25 ml measures of Bacardi were sold in the dispensing bar from a stock of four 75 cl bottles prior to a stock take. How many measures should remain?

– 27 –

Bin cards

For the purposes of ordering and stock-taking it is important for a storekeeper to be able to find out quickly and accurately how much of any item is in stock. There are various methods of doing this but the keeping of 'bin cards' is perhaps the most popular. Although computers are increasingly being used, the principle is the same. The bin card can be attached to the shelf or bin where an item is stored and it is a simple matter for the storekeeper or manager to check the actual stock against the stock shown on the card.

The bin card shown below is a simple form although it is quite easy to add extra information such as 'minimum stock' to warn against running out of a certain item and 'maximum stock' to guard against stock deterioration.

BIN CARD No			
ITEM Flour		Unit .... 1.5 kg	
DATE	RECEIVED	ISSUED	BALANCE
1 Mar	12	3	9
5 Mar		4	5
8 Mar	12	4	13

On 8 March the 12 bags received are added to the 5 bags' balance on 5 March. After issuing 4 bags the final balance is 13 bags, which should equal the number now in stock.

The final balance provides the necessary information to enable the storekeeper to decide whether to reorder and allows the manager to calculate the value of stock held. If flour was valued at £0.42 per kg then the value of the stock of flour on 8 March is £8.19.

Rule out bin cards for the following questions, enter the receipts and issues and find the balance in each case.

1	Sugar	4 April	Received 20 kg	Issued 10 kg
		10 April	Received 20 kg	Issued 5 kg
		15 April		Issued 6 kg
2	Jam	3 Aug	Balance 14	
	(5 kg tin)	6 Aug	Received 6	Issued 2
		10 Aug	Received 6	
3	Peaches	14 Oct	Received 24	
	(Tin)	15 Oct		Issued 3
		18 Oct	Received 12	Issued 4
4	Tea	1 June	Received 14 kg	Issued 1 kg
		2 June		Issued 1 kg
		3 June		Issued 1.5 kg
		4 June		Issued 0.5 kg
		5 June		Issued 1 kg
		6 June	Received 7 kg	Issued 1.75 kg
5	Margarine	3 Mar	Balance 14	
	(250 g)	6 Mar	Received 8	Issued 3
		8 Mar		Issued 2
		10 Mar		Issued 10
		12 Mar	Received 8	
		13 Mar		Issued 5
6	Eggs	4 Jan	Received 120	
		5 Jan		Issued 24
		6 Jan		Issued 30
		7 Jan		Issued 50
		8 Jan	Received 120	Issued 10

— 28 —

Finding the cost of food and drink used – the cost of sales

The food cost of a single dish is usually found by reference to the costing sheet, but to calculate the total food and drink cost of an establishment over a given period it is simpler to use the stock-take and purchases received.

Examples

a The opening food stock on 1 January was £250 and the closing food stock on 31 January was £300. If the food purchases during January amounted to £700, calculate the cost of food used.

Method

Stock on 1 January	£250	Add to find total available
Purchases in January	£700	
	£950	
Stock on 31 January	£300	(subtract unused stock)
Cost of food used	£650	

b Food stock as at 1 Jan – £1,050
Food stock as at 31 Dec – £1,700
Food purchases during year –£10,000
Food purchases returns during year – £500
Calculate the cost of food used.

Method

Stock as at 1 Jan	£1,050	
Purchases less returns	£9,500	(Add)
Total available	£10,550	
Stock as at 31 Dec	£1,700	(Subtract)
Cost of food used	£8,850.	

In the examples above *Purchases* refer to all credit and cash purchases and *Food purchases returns* refer to any returns that have already been included under the heading of *Purchases*. When calculating the value of stock, it is normal practice to take the lower of cost and market price. For example, if a commodity was purchased at 10p per kg and the present price (market price) is 12p per kg then the value of the commodity is calculated at 10p per kg. If the cost price was 15p per kg and the market price is now 11p per kg, the stock is calculated at 11p per kg.

1 Calculate the cost of food used from the following details: opening stock £50, closing stock £25, purchases £40.

2 Find the cost of drink used from the following: stock at 1st January £400, stock at 31st January £450, purchases during January £300.

3 Calculate the food cost from the following: food stock as at 1st January £450, food stock as at 31 December £700. Food purchases during the year £20,000, less food purchases returns £200.

4 Calculate the cost of sales from the following information: opening stock on 1 March £75.50, stock at close of business on 31 March £120.25, purchases made during March £500.75.

5 The books of a small catering unit showed the following statistics for the month of June: opening stock £90, closing stock £100, cash purchases £150, credit purchases £1,350. Calculate the cost of the sales.

6 Find the cost of food used from the following: stock as at 1 December £300, stock as at 31 December £300, local purchases in December £900, supplies from head office in December £150.

7 A business commenced operations on 1 October and during October food purchases amounting to £750 were made. If on 31 October the closing food stock was £85, find the cost of food used.

8 In question 7, what would be the opening stock on 1 November?

9 Calculate the cost of drinks used from the following information: opening stock £908, closing stock £700, purchases £2,000.

10 Find the cost of sales from the following details: stock at 1 January £4,000, stock at 31 December £6,000, purchases during year £10,000.

11 Study the following information: food stock on 1 February £300, stock on 28 February (according to the manager) £350, (according to the storekeeper) £370, purchases during February £645.

a Find the food used (i) according to the manager, (ii) according to the storekeeper.
b Discuss why differences may occur (consider rising and falling prices).

– 29 –

Gross profit and the cost of sales

Gross profit is the difference between the cost of sales (food and drink cost) and the proceeds from sales. It follows that the gross profit is increased or decreased according to the amount of the cost of sales. The following example will demonstrate this statement.

The opening stock of a restaurant was £1,000. Purchases amounted to £5,000. Taking stock at the higher of purchase or market prices gave a closing stock value of £1,500 but taking stock at the lower prices gave a closing stock of £1,350. If the sales over the period were £15,000, calculate the gross profit.

Taking the higher prices		*Taking the lower prices*	
Opening stock	£1,000	Opening stock	£1,000
Purchases	5,000	Purchases	5,000
	6,000		6,000
Closing stock	1,500	Closing stock	1,350
Cost of sales	4,500	Cost of sales	4,650
Sales	£15,000	Sales	£15,000
Cost of sales	4,500	Cost of sales	4,650
Gross profit	£10,500	Gross profit	£10,350

Note how the gross profit was £150 greater by estimating the value of the stock at £150 higher than the lower figure. No extra effort was made by the restaurateur to increase the profit. Of course it did not result in any more money in the restaurateur's pocket – that should be thoroughly understood and is a good point for discussion.

It is now quite understandable why the term 'cost of sales' is used. In achieving sales of £15,000 the *cost* was £4,500 using the higher stock value and £4,650 using the lower value.

1 Find the gross profit from the following statistics:
stock at 1 March £900, stock at 31 March £850, purchases during March £2,400, sales in March £7,500.

2 The following figures were extracted from the books of The Oak Tree Restaurant for a week in May:
opening stock £525, closing stock £600, purchases £2,040, purchases returns £15, sales £5,500.
Calculate **a** the gross profit, **b** the gross profit as a percentage of sales.

3 The stock as at 1 January was £725. Purchases during January amounted to £4,100. The storekeeper estimated the stock on 31 January as £850 but the manager estimated the stock value as £900. The sales in January were £12,500.

- **a** Without making a calculation (if possible) state who would show the higher gross profit.
- **b** Calculate the gross profit according to (i) the storekeeper, (ii) the manager.

4 When buying or selling a business why is it sensible to get an independent expert to value the stock? (For discussion.)

— 30 —

The standard recipe

In a situation where a number of chefs are cooking in the same organisation it is usual to use the *standard recipe.* As its name suggests, it is a method of standardising recipes so that there is a tight control on cost and quantity. Standardisation should not be allowed to stifle the individual chef's flair. It does mean that a Group Catering Manager can control quantities, quality and costs more easily.

The recipe lays down the ingredients, method of production and quantities used. It should give the number of portions to be served – this will determine the size of portion (portion control). A section giving variations can be added to reduce the total number of recipes required.

The advantages in using the standard recipe are:

- **a** A well tried recipe ensures a consistently good finished product.
- **b** It controls portions size, which is so important in costing a dish.
- **c** It is easy to determine the food cost of a particular dish.
- **d** It simplifies the pricing of a particular dish.

e It reduces the possibility of error.

An example of a standard recipe form is shown below.

<table>
<tr><td colspan="3">Recipe...........</td><td colspan="2">No......</td></tr>
<tr><td rowspan="3">Ingredients</td><td colspan="4">Quantities For</td></tr>
<tr><td>25</td><td>50</td><td>100</td><td>200</td></tr>
<tr><td></td><td></td><td></td><td></td></tr>
<tr><td colspan="3">Method of production</td><td colspan="2">Comments</td></tr>
<tr><td colspan="5">Presentation for service</td></tr>
<tr><td>Variations</td><td colspan="4">Variations of ingredients and method</td></tr>
</table>

– 31 –

Costing sheets

Having decided on a particular dish it should be costed out accurately in order to fix the selling price and to find the profit.

A simple costing sheet is set out below.

COSTING SHEET			
Dish		Date	
	Quantity	Unit cost	Total cost
Meat			
Poultry, fish			
Greengrocery			
Dry stores			
Total			
Number of portions			
Cost per portion			

Use the following prices in working out the questions.

baking powder	£3.70 per kg	leeks	£1.55 per kg
beef (topside)	£7.68 per kg	margarine	£0.90 per kg
beer	£2.70 per litre	milk	£0.48 per litre
butter	£3.26 per kg	onions	£0.80 per kg
celery	£1.33 per kg	onions (button)	£1.00 per kg
currants	£2.00 per kg	potatoes	£0.40 per kg
eggs	£1.26 per dozen	suet	£3.08 per kg
flour	£0.46 per kg	sugar (caster)	£0.90 per kg
jam	£1.00 per kg	sugar (granulated)	£0.75 per kg
lamb (stewing)	£3.40 per kg		

Draw costing sheets and find the cost *per portion* of the following. (Work to three decimal places of £.)

1 *Genoese sponge*
(8 portions)

4 eggs
100 g caster sugar
100 g flour
50 g butter

2 *Shortbread biscuits*
(12 portions)

150 g flour
50 g caster sugar
100 g margarine

3 *Steamed currant roll*
(6 portions)

300 g flour
15 g baking powder
75 g gran. sugar
150 g chopped suet
100 g currants

4 *Queen of puddings*
(4 portions)

500 ml milk
100 g caster sugar
25 g butter
50 g jam
3 eggs

5 *Carbonnade of beef*
(4 portions)

400 g lean beef (Topside)
15 g caster sugar
200 g sliced onion
250 ml beer

6 *Irish stew*
(4 portions)

425 g stewing lamb
400 g potatoes
100 g celery
100 g button onions
100 g onions
100 g leeks

— 32 —

Graphs

Graphs can be used effectively to display information in a simple, easy-to-read form. Comparing performance from lists to figures can be time-consuming and may lead to inaccuracies. A graph displayed on a wall can be a permanent reminder of the state of a catering enterprise.

Examine the line graph on the next page.

The horizontal axis A–B refers to the months when a restaurant was in operation.

The vertical axis A–C refers to the sales made by the restaurant each month.

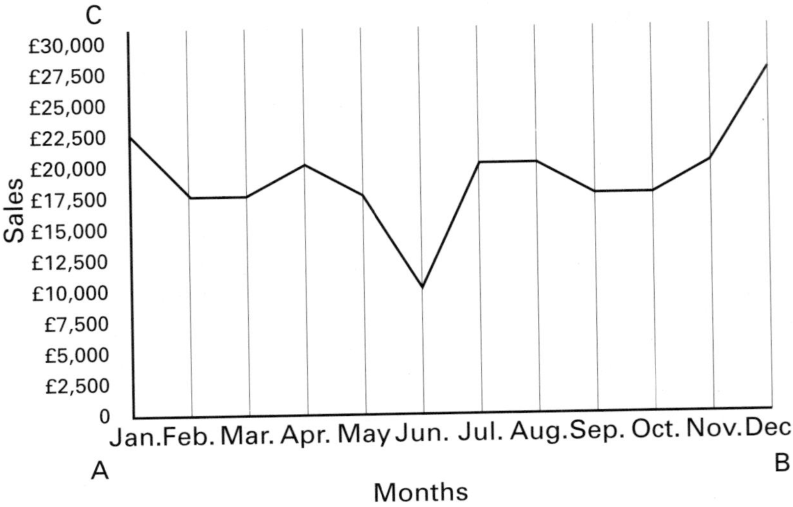

A line graph

To determine the sales for March, first find March on the horizontal axis and then find the plot vertically above. Read the sales figure £17,500 in the left-hand column level with the plot.

Answer the following questions by reference to the graph.

1 What were the sales in July?

2 In which month do you consider the restaurant closed for two weeks?

3 What do you think was the reason for the December sales figure?

Here is an example of a bar chart or block graph. This graph refers to the number of customers served in an industrial canteen during one week.

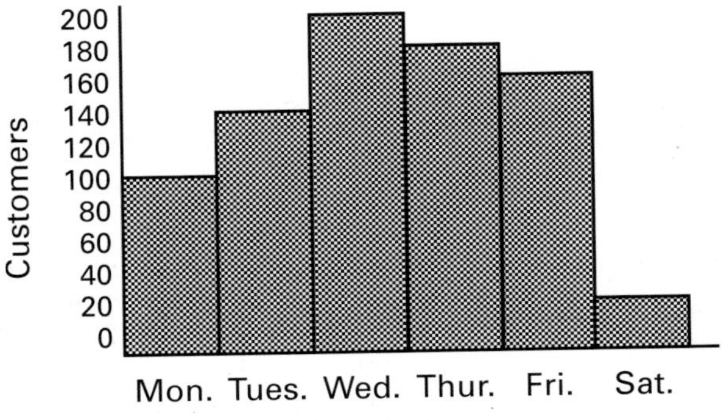

A bar chart

4 How many customers were served on Thursday?

5 Assuming the shape of the graph is typical of every week, on which day can the manageress reduce the staff to minimum cover?

6 On which two days must full staff cover be arranged?

More than one piece of information can be shown on a graph at one time. The following graph shows two sets of facts. The continuous line shows the total sales for each week and the broken line shows the total costs. From these facts we can at a glance determine profit or loss.

The sales in week 1 were £1,700 and the costs £1,500, therefore the net profit was £200.

Notice how easy it is to detect any difference in the net profit from week to week.

7 In week 2:
   a What were the sales?
   b What were the total costs?
   c What was the net profit?

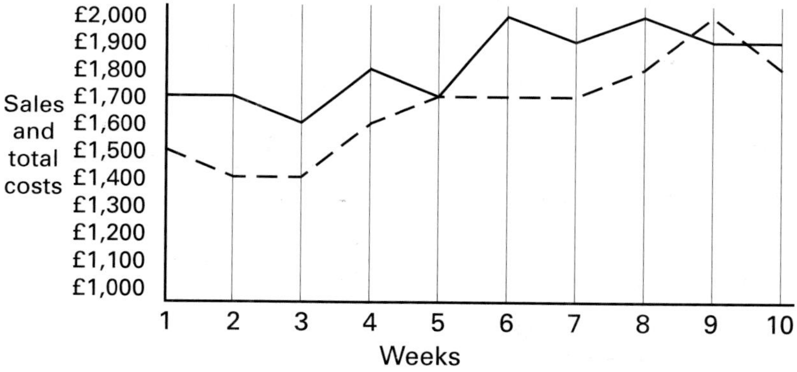

8 What was the net profit in week 6?

9 In which week did the sales equal the costs?

10 In which week was there a net loss?

11 Draw a graph showing the percentage occupancy of a hotel from the following information. Let the horizontal axis represent weeks and the vertical axis represent percentage occupancy.

Week 1: 40% occupancy   Week 2: 50% occupancy
Week 3: 45% occupancy   Week 4: 60% occupancy
Week 5: 75% occupancy.

12 Draw a graph to show the following information:

Month	Jan	Feb	Mar	Apr	May	Jun	Jul	Aug	Sept	Oct	Nov	Dec
No. of customers	400	300	250	300	300	350	300	250	350	350	400	500

13 Using ink to show customers and pencil to show sales, plot the following information on the same graph.

Day	Mon	Tues	Wed	Thurs	Fri	Sat
Customers	50	75	100	75	150	200
Sales	£100	£200	£225	£150	£500	£800

— 33 —

Pie charts

Another way of showing information is by the use of pie charts. Study the following diagrams.

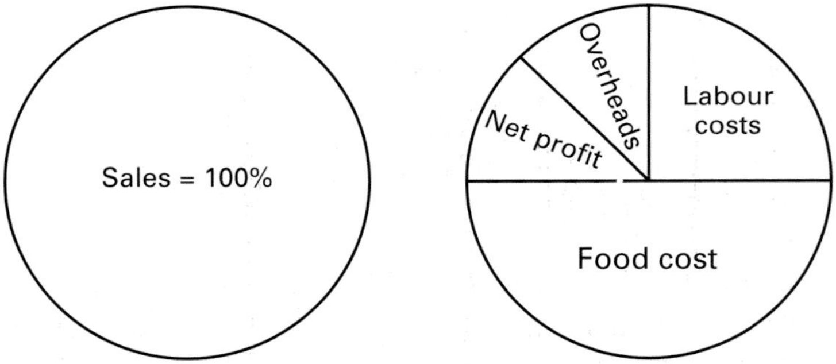

The circle (360°) is divided into segments according to the proportions of costs and profit of a transport café.

In the above example the area of the circle represents the total sales (100%).

The food cost of 50% of sales is represented by 50% of the area or 180° of the circumference (50% of 360°).

The labour costs of 25% of sales are represented by 25% of the area or 90° of the circumference (25% of 360°).

The overheads of 12.5% of sales are represented by 12.5% of the area or 45° of the circumference (12.5% of 360°).

The net profit of 12.5% of sales is similarly represented by 45°.

The chart can be enhanced by showing the various segments in different colours.

1 The following chart shows how the total labour costs of an hotel are divided. Measure the arc of each segment to find the value of each part of the total labour cost of £7,200 per month.

NB First divide the £7,200 by 360 to find the value of 1°.

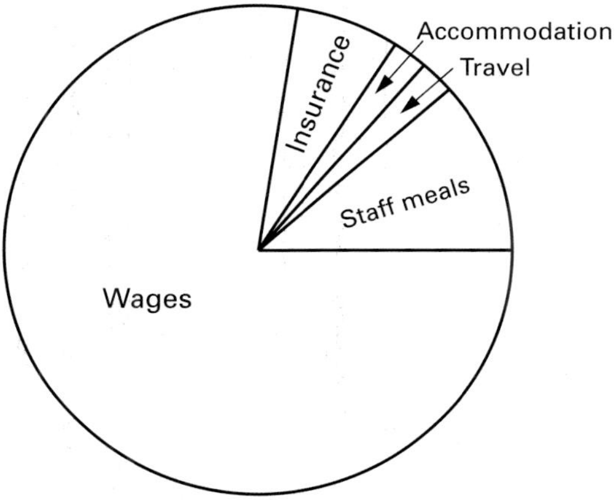

2 Using the following information draw a pie chart to show how each £1 of sales is made up.

Food and drink cost 40% of sales, labour costs 25% of sales, overheads 20% of sales, net profit 15% of sales.

3 The sales of a hotel in one week consisted of accommodation £3,600, food £1,200, drink and tobacco £600.
By means of a pie chart show these items as proportional parts of the total sales.

4 The total sales of a restaurant in one year are shown by the following pie chart. Find the value of each segment if the total sales represented were £360,000.

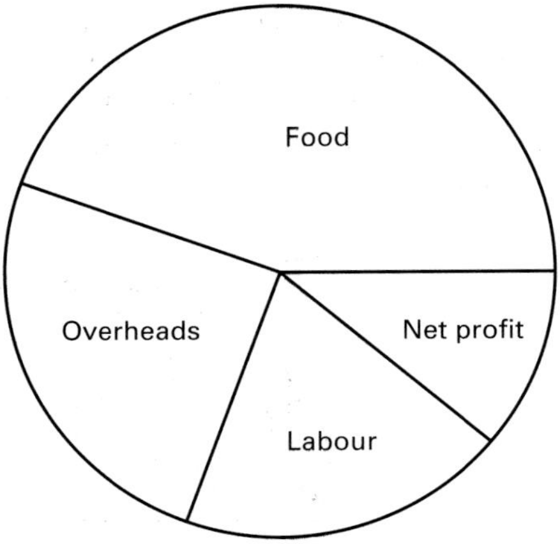

— 34 —

Currency conversion

The hotel and catering trade occupies a very important position in the tourist industry, earning a great deal of foreign currency for Great Britain. In this respect the hotel and catering trade acts as an *export trade* and greatly helps the *balance of trade.*

Foreign visitors mean foreign money and it is therefore sensible to be able to calculate the equivalent values of British and foreign money.

Study the following table.

EXCHANGE RATES FOR £1 STERLING	
Canada	2.03 dollars
France	7.5 francs
Germany	2.25 marks
Italy	2300 lire
Spain	184.13 pesetas
Switzerland	1.80 francs
USA	1.5 dollars

Examples using the above table:

a Calculate the sterling equivalent of 150 French francs

$$\text{if } 7.5 \text{ francs} = £1$$

$$\text{then } 150 \text{ francs} = \frac{150}{7.5} \text{ pounds}$$

$$= £20.$$

b How many French francs are equivalent to £25?

$$\text{if } £1 = 7.5 \text{ francs}$$

$$\text{then } £25 = 25 \times 7.5 \text{ francs}$$

$$= 187.5 \text{ francs.}$$

c How many pounds sterling are equal in value to 300 marks?

$$\text{if } 2.25 = £1$$

$$\text{then } 300 \text{ marks} = \frac{300}{2.25} \text{ pounds}$$

$$= \frac{30\,000}{225}$$

$$= £133.33.$$

Work out the following using the exchange rates in the table provided:

1 How many pounds sterling are equivalent to 1000 US dollars?

2 How many Spanish pesetas are equal in value to £25?

3 A hotel manager agreed to accept 500 French francs in payment of a bill for £46. Calculate the change given to nearest pound.

4 Calculate the equivalent value of £50 in Italian lire.

5 A tourist wished to exchange £500 worth of traveller's cheques for pesetas. Calculate how many pesetas he would receive.

6 A hotel cashed a traveller's cheque for 100 Swiss francs. Calculate the amount of pounds sterling received by the tourist if the hotel deducted 2% commission.

7 How many Canadian dollars are equal to £200?

8 How many Swiss francs should be obtained for £15?

9 How many pesetas should be requested from a potential Spanish tourist if a hotel required the equivalent of £20 deposit for a postal booking? (Ans. to nearest 100 pts.)

10 A hotel offers to buy French francs at 9 francs to the £ but sells French francs at 7.5 francs to the £.

a A tourist wishes to cash 135 francs into £ sterling. How many pounds would the tourist receive?

b A Frenchman returning home wishes to change £15 into francs. How many francs will he receive?

— 35 —

Twenty-four hour clock

An increase in the foreign tourist trade and closer links with the Continent mean that there is an increasing use of the 24-hour clock system. Bus, train, boat and air timetables now use the 24-hour clock because this method helps to stop confusion over arrival and departure times.

Here are a few examples showing the same times for the 12-hour and 24-hour systems.

12-hour	*24-hour*
9 a.m.	09.00
10.30 a.m.	10.30
1.45 p.m.	13.45
8 p.m.	20.00

Notice that in the 24-hour system all times are calculated from midnight and all times are represented by four figures (two figures for hours and two figures for minutes). Sometimes the word 'hours' is written after the figures, e.g. 14.25 hours.

Change the following to the 24-hour clock system:

1	5 a.m.	**2**	12.25 p.m.	**3**	10 p.m.	**4**	2.10 a.m.
5	11.27 a.m.	**6**	midday	**7**	11.55 p.m.	**8**	3 p.m.

Change the following to the 12-hour-clock system:

9	03.00	**10**	17.30	**11**	00.15	**12**	16.00
13	22.20	**14**	11.28	**15**	20.05	**16**	13.00

Use the 24-hour clock in working out the following questions:

17 A dish that takes $2\frac{1}{2}$ hours to cook was placed in the oven at 16.35 hours. At what time will the dish be ready to serve?

18 At 10.40 hours a hotel receptionist took a phone message to say that a guest would be arriving in 4 hours' time. At what time would the guest be expected to arrive?

19 A dish takes 3 hours 25 minutes to cook. At what time must the dish be placed in the oven in order to be ready to serve by 13.15 hours?

20 A guest requests a receptionist to find the time of arrival of a boat in Le Havre. The timetable shows that the boat leaves Portsmouth at 10.20 hours and takes $5\frac{1}{2}$ hours to cross the channel. If the French authorities add 1 hour to British time (to conserve energy), at what time will the boat arrive in France?

21 Four dishes must be ready 15 minutes before the time of serving. Find the starting time for cooking each dish if they are to be served at 20.00 hours and they take the following cooking times:

Dish A, $1\frac{1}{2}$ hours	Dish B, 2 hours 10 minutes
Dish C, 45 minutes	Dish D, 1 hour 20 minutes.

22 A hotel is to arrange for a guest to be met by car at an airport. If the flight leaves Germany at 23.04 (UK time) and takes $1\frac{3}{4}$ hours, at what time should the car be at the airport?

23 A telephone call was logged in at an hotel at 2 minutes past midnight. Write this time according to the 24-hour clock.

Mixed tests

Test 1

1 Find the total week's taking of a café if the daily receipts were:

Monday, £150.12	Tuesday, £148.08
Wednesday, £250.90	Thursday, £47.03
Friday, £184.75	Saturday, £215.15.

2 If question 1 referred to a week when the cost of food and drink was £328.34, calculate the gross profit.

3 The average weekly wage bill for an industrial canteen was £308.32. Calculate the total wages paid in one year.

4 The total ingredient cost for 25 covers was £31.70. Find the cost per cover to the nearest penny.

5 **a** Find 40% of £300.
b Allowing 35% wastage in preparation and cooking, calculate the weight of meat remaining to be served from a delivery of 40 kg.

6 Find the cost of buying 50 kg of sugar at £0.75 per kg.

7 During one day the sales amounted to £347.57. What was the net profit if the food cost was £120.50, the labour costs were £95.72 and the overheads cost was £92.05?

8 Cancel **a** $\frac{34}{51}$ **b** $\frac{14}{84}$ **c** $\frac{150}{1000}$

9 Find the arithmetic mean of:
25, 16, 33, 41, 15, 20.

10 Find the cost of 600 ml if 1 litre costs 25p.

Test 2

1 Total the following bill.

4 kg	at £0.09 per kg
1.5 kg	at £0.32 per kg
4.125 litres	at £0.80 per litre
150 g	at £1.00 per kg

2 Find the food cost for March from the following figures:

opening food stock as at 1 March	£205
closing food stock as at 31 March	£293
food purchases during March	£348.

3 Find the floor area of a room 6 m in length by 5 m wide.

4 Find the total receipts if the following amounts of money were taken during one day:

$4 \times$ £10, $7 \times$ £5, $14 \times$ £1, $23 \times$ 50p, $20 \times$ 10p, $18 \times$ 5p, $45 \times$ 2p, $52 \times$ 1p.

5 Find the cost of buying 3 kg if 25 g cost £0.04.

6 If the total sales were £550, express each of the following as a percentage of sales:

meat £60, vegetables £38, sweets £40, tea and coffee £7.

7 Express 4372 g in kilograms.

8 An analysis of the cash register showed that 1200 customers spent £1,350. How much did the average customer spend?

9 If £32 represents 12% of an amount, find 39%.

10 From 2 litres of cooking oil, 175 ml was absorbed. What percentage of the original amount was absorbed?

Test 3

1 The following details were taken from the books of The Stag Hotel:
food cost £305.00, labour cost £275.00, overheads cost £225.00, sales £900.00.

Calculate: **a** the gross profit as a percentage of sales;
b the net profit as a percentage of sales.

2 One hundred 125 g portions of meat are required to be served. Allowing 40% for wastage, calculate how many kg of meat should be ordered (to nearest kg).

3 The original price of goods bought by a caterer was £83.50. He was allowed a trade discount of 20%. Calculate the amount paid by the caterer.

4 Express the following ratio in the most simplified form:
56:48:104

5 If the food cost of a dish was £0.34, calculate the price that should be charged for this dish in order to achieve a profit of 65% on the selling price.

6 A dish was priced at £1.05 and the food cost of the dish was £0.35. Find the gross profit as a percentage of the selling price.

7 Find the cost of sales during June from the following details:
stocks at 1 June £205.00, stock at 30 June £180.00,
credit purchases £508.00, cash purchases £28.00, purchases returns £15.00.

8 A hotel has 65 bedrooms. If 26 bedrooms are not occupied, what is the percentage occupancy?

9 The food and beverages cost of an industrial canteen during one 5-day week was £800. If daily receipts from sales were £130, calculate the subsidy per meal if on average 200 meals were served.

10 **a** Find the sales from 10000 cups of coffee sold at £0.75 per cup.
b If the sales from 2000 meals totalled £9,100 find the average charge per meal.

Test 4

1 The following are the costs of a dish to produce 20 portions.

4 kg at £1.50 per kg
2.5 kg at £1.06 per kg
200 g at £0.75 per kg

a Calculate the cost per cover.
b (i) Find the selling price per cover to achieve a profit of 60% on the selling price.
(ii) Find the gross profit per cover.
c Using your answer for **a** above, find the profit as a percentage of the selling price if the selling price was £1.50 per cover.

2 The following statistics were taken from the book of The Sea View Hotel:

	£
Stock at 1 February	316
Stock at 8 February	350
Purchases during 1–8 February	410
Sales	1000

a Find the cost of sales. (Food and drink cost.)
b Calculate the gross profit as a percentage of sales.

3 For a lunch for 100 guests the charge per head is £8.90.
Gross profit is 55% of sales. Labour costs are £211.50. Overhead cost is £190.
Find: **a** the food cost for 100 covers;
b the net profit per cover.

4 The manager of a works canteen covers all expenses when charging for the 200 meals he produces each day for 5 days a week.
If the food cost amounts to £2,000 per week and labour and overheads amount to £1,250 per week, calculate the average selling price per meal.

5 A canteen assistant earns £3.56 per hour. Calculate the gross wage earned in a 5-day week if the assistant works from 9 a.m. until 4.30 p.m., with a break of 1 hour for lunch.

6 Find the cost of 75 g if 1 kilogram costs £1.60.

Test 5

1 Draw a graph to represent the following information:

Sales	£8,500	£8,000	£8,600	£8,600	£8,500	£8,900	£9,000	£8,900	£8,800	£8,900	£9,000	£9,000
Months	Jan	Feb	Mar	Apr	May	Jun	July	Aug	Sept	Oct	Nov	Dec

2 The following statistics were extracted from the books of a catering establishment during February:
meat cost £1,232, vegetables cost £740, dry goods cost £836, beverages cost £292, sales £8,000.

a Express each cost as a percentage of the sales.
b A check in March revealed the meat cost to be 20% of sales. Give possible reasons for this increase.

3 **a** Find the cost of 5.125 kg at £0.12 per kg.
b Find the cost of 375 g at £3.00 per kg.

4 If the budgeted sales were £5,000 less than the actual sales and the budgeted costs were £1,000 greater than the actual costs, how would that effect the budgeted profit or loss?

5 A caterer ordered and received 50 kg of meat costing £6.00 per kg.

a If 37.5% was wasted in preparation and cooking, how many portions each of 125 g can be produced?
b Calculate the cost per portion to the caterer.

6 The following figures were taken from the books of The Chestnut Restaurant during the first week of July:

	£
Food cost	2,400
Full-time labour costs	1,620
Part-time labour costs	300
Rates	630
Power	525
Renewals	144
Advertising	105
Telephone	75
Stationery	45
Sales	7,200

Find as a percentage of sales:

a the gross profit
b the net profit
c the labour costs
d the total costs.

Test 6

1 The total food cost of a dinner for 40 guests was £243.44. If the labour costs are reckoned at £152.20 and the overheads estimated at 25% of sales, calculate the charge per cover to give a net profit of 12% on sales.

2 One hundred and twelve 125 g portions of meat are required to be served.
   a If 30% is allowed for wastage, find how many kg of meat must be ordered.
   b If the cost price of the meat is £6.16 per kg, find the gross profit as a percentage of the selling price assuming each portion is sold for £3.00.

3 The price of a stores order was £35.05. If the discount allowed was 15%, calculate the amount paid.

4 Write the following amounts to the nearest penny:

   a £14.0148 **b** £25.17841 **c** £0.845.

5 From a delivery of 275 kg of potatoes, 15.5 kg were found to be unusable. What percentage of the delivery could be used?

6 The total takings of a café during one week were as follows:

Monday £151.20	Tuesday £166.10	Wednesday £208
Thursday £161.50	Friday £250.88	Saturday £416.30

   a Calculate the gross profit as a percentage of sales if the food and drink costs were £405 and the VAT payable on the sales was £195.
   b During the week there were 770 customers. How much did the average customer spend (to nearest penny)?
   c In the next week there was a 20% increase in customers and the average customer spent £1.80. Find the total takings for the week.

7 A storage tank with a base of 12 square metres had a depth of 1.5 metres. Find the volume of this tank.

Test 7

1 Write the following amounts corrected to 2 decimal places of £1.

a £0.1782 **b** £14.205 **c** £0.87477.

2 Draw a bin card, enter the following details and show the balance at the end of the week:

Item: Jam Unit:kg		
3 July	Balance 10	
4 July	Received 5	Issued 3
5 July		Issued 2
6 July	Received 10	
7 July		Issued 6
8 July	Received 5	Issued 3

3 The following figures were taken from the books of The Elizabethan Restaurant:

	£
Food stock at 1 January	610
Food stock at 31 January	804
Cash purchases during January	270
Credit purchases during January	25,000
Purchases returns during January	90
Sales during January	60,000

a Calculate (i) the food cost during January, (ii) the gross profit during January.
b What was the opening food stock at 1 February?

4 In setting a business rate, the valuation officer (representing the Inland Revenue) considers local rents of similar establishments, together with the floor area of the business to be rated.

The diagram below shows the internal measurements of a cafe.

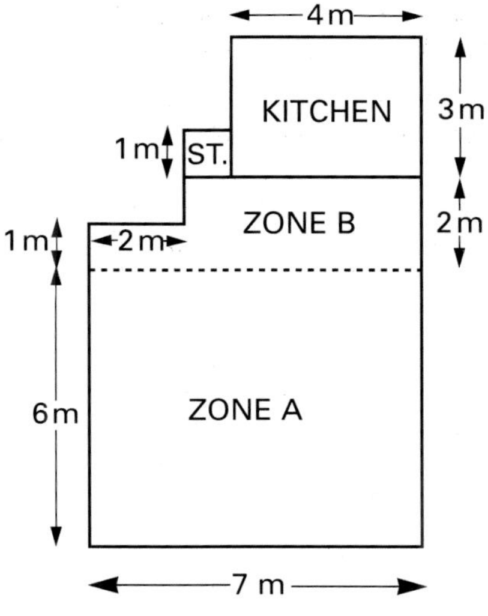

The first 6 metres (zone A), is valued in this case at £115 per square metre. Zone B refers to the next 6 metres (or up to the next 6 metres), but excludes specified areas such as toilets, stores, offices and kitchens. Zone B is valued at half the zone A rate. The stores and kitchen are valued at £30 per square metre.

a Calculate the total rateable value the valuation officer places on the cafe. (Answer to nearest £100).

b If the government sets a business rate of £0.40 (to pay) for every £1 of rateable value, use your answer to **a** to find how much will be paid by the owner of the café in one year.

5 Express **a** 3 kg 25 g in grams **b** 7148 g in kg **c** 4.25 litres in ml **d** 6 litres 35 ml in litres.

6 Share £30,000 in the ratio of 8:7.

Test 8

1 **a** What are 'the elements of cost?
b Under which element of cost would you place:
(i) gas (ii) staff meals (iii) meat (iv) depreciation (v) telephone?

2 A cook requires 17 kg of meat on the plates. Allowing 32% for wastage, **a** how much meat should be ordered? **b** What will be the cost at £5.80 per kg?

3 A hotel had 20 double bedrooms at £42.50 per person and 30 single bedrooms at £52.00 per person. 13 double bedrooms and 18 single bedrooms were fully occupied.
a Find the percentage occupancy of (i) the double bedrooms, (ii) the single bedrooms, (iii) the hotel as a whole.
b If the total sales for the day were £2,700, calculate the receipts from the apartments as a percentage of the total sales.

4 The following figures were taken from the books of The Sea View Restaurant:

	£
Food cost	3,900
Full-time labour	2,460
Part-time labour	300
Rent and rates	1,320
Telephone	180
Gas and electricity	936
Insurance	168
Depreciation and renewals	192
Advertising	138
Sales	11,700

Find **a** the gross profit as a percentage of sales
b the net profit as a percentage of sales
c the overheads as a percentage of sales.

5 If £2.50 was required for a dish in order to give a 60% profit on sales before the addition of VAT, calculate the price a customer must pay if the rate of VAT was:
a 15% **b** 17.5% **c** 20% (answers to nearest penny).

6 A domestic assistant's hours of work were as follows: Monday 9 a.m.–6 p.m., Tuesday 8.30 a.m.–5 p.m., Wednesday 8.30 a.m.–5.30 p.m., Thursday 9 a.m.–6 p.m., Friday 8.30 a.m.–5 p.m. Calculate the assistant's wages per week if the hourly rate of pay was £3.25 for the first 37 hours worked and £3.65 per hour for any hours worked in excess of 37. (Allow 1 hour per day for lunch.)

Test 9

1 During one week a caterer makes £555 gross profit, which was 60% of sales. Labour costs were £225 and overheads £240.
- **a** Find (i) the sales, (ii) the net profit, (iii) the net profit as a percentage of sales.
- **b** If the labour costs had been £280 and the overheads £290, what is the term given to the net figure?

2 At the end of a six-month period it was found that food costs had increased by 5% and yet the gross profit percentage had remained at 65% of sales. How was this possible if the following assumptions are made?
- (i) There was no decrease in wastage.
- (ii) Portion size had remained constant.
- (iii) There had never been any pilfering.

3 The stock records of a catering establishment showed the following details for the month of February:

Opening food stock on 1 February	£705
Food purchases	£510

The closing food stock was valued at £800 by the storekeeper but at £775 by the manager.
The sales during February were £1,300.

- **a** Calculate the food cost in February (i) according to the storekeeper, (ii) according to the manager.
- **b** Calculate the gross profit as a percentage of sales (i) according to the storekeeper, (ii) according to the manager.
- **c** Give possible reasons for this difference and discuss the fairness of valuing stock at the lower of cost or market price in times of inflation.

4 A school meals service produces 10000 meals each day on 5 days per week for 40 weeks in a year. The total food costs are £2,100,000, labour and overheads amount to £100,000 per year.
  a Calculate the food cost per meal.
  b If the charge per meal is £1, find the subsidy paid on each meal.

5 From the information shown in the table below, plot the two sets of information on one graph.

Day	Mon	Tues	Wed	Thurs	Fri	Sat
Customers	50	60	60	45	75	95
Sales	£115	£120	£150	£80	£225	£285

6 Write down the advantage to a catering group of introducing the 'standard recipe'.

Test 10

1 **a** A caterer was asked to plan a buffet for 50 guests each paying £5.25. The labour costs were estimated to be: full-time £45.00 and part-time £20.00. Overheads are reckoned as 20% of sales. Calculate how much can be spent on food per cover if a net profit of 10% on sales is required.
  b New food prices show there is an increase of 10p per cover. The management decide to keep the same menu and not to increase the charge for the buffet. Calculate the net profit percentage of sales using the new prices.

2 A restaurateur uses 125 ml as his standard wine measurement. He buys Chardonnay at £4.20 per 75 cl bottle and requires to achieve a gross profit of 60% on the selling price. Ignoring the effect of VAT:
  a Calculate
    (i) the price per bottle he must charge.
    (ii) the price per glass he must charge.
  b Find the gross profit as a percentage of the selling price if he sold the wine at £1.80 per glass.

3 The following figures were taken from the books of The Blue Bell Restaurant:

	£
Stock at 1 August	528.00
Stock at 15 August	256.00
Purchases during August	7,000.00
Purchases returns in August	50.00
Labour cost – full-time	4,634.00
part-time	1,024.00
Rent and rates	1,660.00
Depreciation	610.00

Postage and stationery	323.00
Telephone	729.00
Insurance	520.00
Gas and electricity	972.00
Advertising	453.00
Sales	21,000.00

Find

a the gross profit as a percentage of sales
b the net profit as a percentage of sales
c the labour cost as a percentage of sales
d the total costs as a percentage of sales. (Try to work this out by studying the answer to **b**.)

4 The daily occupancy of a hotel capable of sleeping 50 guests was as follows:

Mon	Tues	Wed	Thurs	Fri	Sat	Sun
20	36	28	25	35	48	15

What was the percentage occupancy for the week?

Test 11

1 An industrial canteen manager aimed to make a gross profit of 55% on sales. The figures for the first month showed that out of sales of £5,000 the gross profit was 48% on sales.

a By how much money did the actual sales differ from the required sales? (To the nearest £.)
b On closer examination it was found that the food costs included the cost of staff meals, which amounted to £400. Give the corrected gross profit as a percentage of sales.

2 Restaurant *A* made a profit of £30,000, giving a net profit of 10% on sales. Over the same period Restaurant *B* made a net profit of £40,000, which gave a net profit of 8% on sales. If the capital invested in each business was identical, which restaurant was the more successful? (For discussion.)

3 A caterer required to serve two hundred 125 g portions of meat. If he bought from supplier *A* at £5.40 per kg, an allowance of 40% should be made for wastage. If he bought from supplier *B* at £6.20 per kg, an allowance of 35% should be made for wastage.

a If supplier *A* was selected, how many kg of meat should be ordered? (Answer to nearest kg)
b If supplier *B* was selected, how many kg of meat should be ordered? (Answer to nearest kg)
c Which is the better buy (on the information given)?
d Discuss other factors that should be taken into account.

4 R. Bryon commenced business on 1 January. The following details relate to his food purchases and sales in the first two months.

		£		
10 Jan	Purchases	3,000	Sales during January	£7,000
31 Jan	Closing Stock	500		
5 Feb	Purchases	2,000	Sales during February	£8,300
23 Feb	Purchases	1,400		
28 Feb	Closing Stock	750		

a Calculate the cost of food in (i) January (ii) February.
b Calculate the gross profit in (i) January (ii) February.

Test 12

1 A catering manager aimed to make a gross profit of 65% on sales. The £3,750 food sales for one week showed a gross profit of 60% on sales and a net profit of 10% on sales.
a What was the actual food cost?
b What should the sales have been in order to achieve the aim of the manager? (To nearest £)
c If the labour cost was £1,000, express the overhead cost as a percentage of the actual sales.

2 The following ingredients are required to produce 8 portions of Spaghetti Bolognaise:

Spaghetti	250 g at £0.76 per kg
Parmesan cheese	100 g at £4.85 per 250 g
Stewing beef	200 g at £4.50 per kg
Onions	100 g at £0.90 per kg
Butter	25 g at £3.28 per kg
Garlic	10 g at a cost of £0.05
Jus lie	250 ml estimated cost £0.10

a Find the total ingredient cost *per portion* (to nearest penny).
b Find the selling price per portion to achieve a 60% profit on sales.
c If the selling price was £1.00 per portion, express the profit as a percentage of sales.

3 The following statistics were taken from the books of the Waterside Hotel:

	£
Food stock at 1 Feb.	820
Food stock at 6 Feb.	1,068
Food purchases	1,684
Food purchases returns	16
Labour cost	1,100
Rent and rates	480

Telephone	50
Power	276
Stationery	36
Advertising	50
Depreciation and renewals	40
Insurance	76
Sales	4,200

Find: **a** food cost; **b** gross profit as a percentage of sales; **c** net profit as a percentage of sales.

4 You have been asked to plan a dinner for 50 guests paying £12.50 per head. The labour cost is estimated to be: full-time, £120.00; part-time, £30.00. Overheads are reckoned as 20% of sales. Calculate how much can be spent on food per cover if a net profit of 10% on sales is required.

Test 13

1 The following costs and sales refer to two differing types of catering establishments. One is a high-class restaurant and the other a self-service cafeteria.

	A	*B*
	£	£
Food	1,050	700
Labour	870	480
Overheads	896	492
Sales	3,200	1,900

a Calculate as a percentage of sales for each establishment:
(i) gross profit (ii) labour cost
(iii) overheads (iv) net profit.

b Say with reasons which you consider to be the high-class restaurant.

2 How can an increase in sales increase the net profit as a percentage of sales without necessarily increasing the gross profit as a percentage of sales? (For discussion.)

3 A chef served forty-eight 125 g portions of meat and charged £5.25 per portion. The meat cost the chef £6.10 per kg and an allowance of 40% was made for wastage.
Find: **a** the total cost of the meat to the chef,
b the gross profit as a percentage of the selling price.

4 The Falcon Hotel has 75 double rooms and 50 single rooms. The charge for a double room is £75 and for a single room £50. The guests' tabular ledger showed the following rooms fully occupied:

	Mon	Tues	Wed	Thurs	Fri	Sat	Sun
Double rooms	40	40	30	35	50	60	45
Single rooms	30	40	50	50	50	25	25

Calculate: **a** the total receipts from rooms for the week.
b the actual guest occupancy as a percentage of the possible guest occupancy.
c plot both sets of figures (double and single rooms) on the same graph.

Test 14

1 The bursar of a college hall of residence hoped to cover all expenses during a year of 52 weeks. The normal college year was of 30 weeks' duration. Income from students amounted to £3,500 per week during term time. Expenses were as follows:

Food and beverages – £1,400 per week during term time
Labour and overheads – £1,345 per week for the full 52 weeks.

There was a chance of three conferences of equal length being held at the hall during vacations, accommodating 30, 45 and 40 persons respectively. The cost of food and beverages for these conferences would be £30 per head.

a Calculate to the nearest £1 the quote per person that the bursar should give to the conference organiser in order to cover all expenses for the year.
b The conference organiser replies that he will only take the hall at £75 per person. Should the bursar accept this offer if there is no possibility of other bookings? (Give figures to support your answer.)
c If the bursar accepted the terms, calculate the expected costs to be covered for the year as a percentage of the total costs.

2 The books of a catering company showed the following facts:

	£
Food stock at 1 June	506
Food stock at 30 June	610
Food purchases in June	19,500
Food purchases returns	25
Sales in June	50,250

The expected gross profit was 65% of sales.
Calculate: **a** the food cost during June
b the actual gross profit as a percentage of sales
c the difference between the actual and expected gross profit. (To the nearest £)

3 A caterer required the following profit on his receipts: on dish A – 60%, on dish B – 50%, on dish C – 65%.

The food costs of the dishes are: A – £0.70, B – £1.25, C – £1.75. Allowing for VAT rate of 17.5%, what must be the charge for each dish? (Answers to nearest penny.)

4 Consider the question and answer to **1b** in discussing the following: 'Is it advantageous under certain circumstances to sell a dish that will give a net loss but a gross profit?'

5 The bill for a group of diners comprised of £66 for food and £18 for drinks. If VAT at 17.5% had been included in this bill, calculate the amount exclusive of VAT retained by the restaurant. (Ans. to nearest penny.)

Multiple choice questions

1 What is 14.1348 corrected to 2 decimal places?
a 14.13
b 14.15
c 14.135
d 14.14

2 What is the total cost of 3000 cakes at 9p each?
a £27.00
b £0.270
c £2700.00
d £270.00

3 Which formula is used to calculate the cubic capacity of a water tank?
a Length × Breadth
b Length × Breadth × Depth
c Area of the base ÷ Depth
d Depth × Length

4 Over a year the sales in a hotel were as follows: restaurant £100,000, bar £20,000, accommodation £1,200,500.
What is the ratio of sales in the restaurant to the bar to the accommodation, expressed in the lowest terms?
a 100000 : 20000 : 1200500
b 200 : 40 : 2401
c 100 : 200 : 1200
d 2401 : 200 : 40

5 On one night a hotel with a capacity to sleep 250 had 35 guests. How is the percentage occupancy calculated?
a $\frac{35}{100} \times \frac{50}{1}$
b $\frac{250}{35} \times \frac{100}{1}$
c $\frac{35}{250} \times \frac{100}{1}$
d $\frac{250}{100} \times \frac{35}{1}$

6 What is a break-even point?
a when the total costs are equal to the total sales.
b when a net profit is achieved.
c when sales are greater than costs.
d when food/drink costs equal the sales.

7 What term is used when the food costs are deducted from the sales?
a net profit
b food cost percentage
c gross profit
d labour and overheads

8 An oven which cost £4,500 is fully depreciated over ten years. What is its value after three years?
a £450
b £4,050
c £3,600
d £3,150

9 What would be the result if the cost of staff meals was included in the total food cost?
a an increase in gross profit.
b an increase in net profit.
c no change in net profit.
d no change in gross profit.

10 A cafe owner arranges 14 of the 20 tables in a 'No smoking' area. What percentage of the tables are in the 'Smoking' area?
a 70%
b 6%
c 30%
d 3%

11 Which term is applied to the 'discount' offered by a supplier to encourage a customer to pay promptly?
a trade discount
b net discount
c credit discount
d cash discount

12 An analysis of a lunch-time trade showed the following sales: 2 @ £3, 8 @ £2, 5 @ £6, 1 @ £12. Which represents the model amount?
a £12
b £3
c £2
d £6

13 A caterer requires a profit of 50% on the selling price for a dish costing £4.80 to produce. What is the selling price?
a £7.20
b £14.40
c £2.40
d £9.60

14 A stock analysis showed the following details:
Opening stock – £500, Closing stock – £825, Purchases – £1,000, Purchase returns – £50. What was the 'cost of sales'?

a £225
b £625
c £1,275
d £675

15 The takings in a restaurant for one week were £7,200 inclusive of VAT at 17.5%. To find how much money the owner will retain, which figure (divisor) should be divided into the £7,200?

a 17.5
b 117.5
c 1.175
d 0.175

16 What best describes 'budgeting'?

a an action based on past performance and future estimates.
b a delayed decision – wait and see what happens.
c a consideration of past figures plus the addition of a fixed percentage.
d a disregard of the past and a guess at future requirements.

17 A bank sells francs at 7 to the pound, but buys francs at 9 to the pound. How would the bank calculate the number of pounds it would exchange for 60 francs?

a $\frac{60}{9}$

b $\frac{60}{7}$

c 7×60

d $\frac{9}{60}$

18 Out of the total food costs of £1,000, the meat cost £200. What is the meat cost expressed as a percentage of the total costs?

a 200%
b 5%
c 20%
d 8%

Answers to exercises

1 *Addition (page 1)*

1	1344	**2**	2182	**3**	12009	**4**	10499
5	10038	**6**	11172	**7**	9111	**8**	9347
9	60.55	**10**	132.09	**11**	518.95	**12**	760.87
13	64.32	**14**	898.94	**15**	803.74	**16**	1233.43
17	£144.49	**18**	£573.86	**19**	£189.93	**20**	£459.62
21	46.37 kg	**22**	230.62 kg	**23**	246.04 litres	**24**	45.09 litres
25	49.91	**26**	99.71	**27**	477.58	**28**	£65.11
29	£987.84	**30**	£23.29	**31**	£2.42	**32**	£53.41
33	£394.70	**34**	£2,160.41	**35**	7.425 kg	**36**	18.35 kg
37	125.025 kg	**38**	68.005 kg	**39**	6.175 litres	**40**	25.34 litres
41	130.042 litres	**42**	7.006 litres	**43**	£16.415	**44**	£22.023
45	£36.338	**46**	£728.119	**47**	169.353 kg	**48**	69.047 kg
49	117.553 litres	**50**	157.598 litres				

2 *Subtraction (page 3)*

1	356	**2**	1138	**3**	3328	**4**	5505
5	£14.58	**6**	£16.78	**7**	£291.79	**8**	£464.82
9	4.95 kg	**10**	16.828 kg	**11**	7.77 kg	**12**	54.975 kg
13	5.924 litres	**14**	75.824 litres	**15**	31.979 litres	**16**	16.678 litres
17	£12.15	**18**	£35.72	**19**	£40.90	**20**	£9.28
21	£7.516	**22**	£0.522	**23**	4.5 kg	**24**	45.075 kg
25	4.74 kg	**26**	7.198 kg	**27**	71.8 litres	**28**	10.5 litres
29	3.875 litres	**30**	76.9 litres	**31**	£361.30	**32**	2.484 kg
33	£28.68	**34**	21.375 litres				

3 *Multiplication (page 4)*

1	18	**2**	40	**3**	28	**4**	30
5	72	**6**	132	**7**	32	**8**	84
9	27	**10**	48	**11**	81	**12**	48
13	121	**14**	42	**15**	36	**16**	20
17	64	**18**	60	**19**	36	**20**	144
21	870	**22**	2569	**23**	3264	**24**	4000
25	32994	**26**	72182	**27**	103.8	**28**	338.48
29	74.82	**30**	£50.58	**31**	£72.45	**32**	£126.80
33	£4,940.46	**34**	£4,007.64	**35**	£75.70	**36**	£34.20
37	£183.664	**38**	£1,053.132	**39**	£5.00	**40**	£93.24
41	£33.80	**42**	31.375 kg	**43**	17.712 kg	**44**	206.25 kg
45	2767.5 kg	**46**	603.96 kg	**47**	4039 kg	**48**	121.5 litres
49	55.65 litres	**50**	156.25 litres	**51**	£43.20	**52**	£1,465.00
53	£140.00	**54**	56.4 kg	**55**	2105 litres	**56**	16125 kg

4 *Division (page 6)*

1	8	**2**	12	**3**	5	**4**	8
5	6	**6**	8	**7**	10	**8**	9
9	6	**10**	9	**11**	7	**12**	9
13	11	**14**	7	**15**	3	**16**	7
17	6	**18**	9	**19**	5	**20**	7
21	206	**22**	509	**23**	146	**24**	459
25	504	**26**	65	**27**	4205	**28**	731

29	265	**30**	809	**31**	109	**32**	2901
33	17	**34**	185	**35**	73	**36**	4.15
37	2.81	**38**	20.5	**39**	123	**40**	32
41	1.5	**42**	12.62	**43**	1.3475	**44**	4.45
45	2.14	**46**	0.452	**47**	1.485	**48**	4.3
49	12.9	**50**	17.7	**51**	9.242	**52**	0.655
53	1.775	**54**	£2.54	**55**	4.642 kg	**56**	£2.49
57	£12.85	**58**	2.623 litres	**59**	£21.85	**60**	6.24
61	£1.638	**62**	4.375 kg	**63**	14.3	**64**	1.827
65	18.497	**66**	£49.13	**67**	22 kg	**68**	17.94
69	3.33	**70**	£6.467	**71**	1.432	**72**	£0.3642
73	£112.36	**74**	4.5 kg	**75**	4.103 litres	**76**	0.525 litres

5 Problems using the four rules (page 9)

1 Butter £13.04, sugar £6.00, flour £1.15, ginger £1.40, vinegar £3.15, *total* £24.74.

2 43p **3** **a** £0.76 **b** £0.77 **4** £128.50

5 **a** £125 **b** £0.85 **6** 15 **7** 200

6 Area and volume (page 10)

1 60 sq m **2** 4 m **3** £3,375 **4** 138.5 sq m

5 **a** 4.3 m **b** £500 **6** 120 cu m **7** 2.5 m **8** **a** yes **b** 48 cu m

9 112500 litres

7 Cancelling (page 13)

1	$\frac{8}{9}$	**2**	$\frac{1}{2}$	**3**	$\frac{7}{9}$	**4**	$\frac{3}{4}$
5	$\frac{7}{12}$	**6**	$\frac{1}{3}$	**7**	$\frac{4}{5}$	**8**	$\frac{1}{4}$
9	$\frac{3}{4}$	**10**	$\frac{1}{4}$	**11**	$\frac{1}{3}$	**12**	$\frac{4}{5}$

8 Mixed numbers and improper fractions (page 14)

1	$\frac{9}{2}$	**2**	$\frac{12}{5}$	**3**	$\frac{29}{4}$	**4**	$\frac{35}{6}$
5	$\frac{32}{3}$	**6**	$\frac{29}{15}$	**7**	$\frac{15}{4}$	**8**	$\frac{16}{7}$
9	$\frac{35}{8}$	**10**	$\frac{203}{10}$	**11**	$1\frac{1}{6}$	**12**	$2\frac{2}{3}$
13	$3\frac{1}{8}$	**14**	$2\frac{2}{11}$	**15**	$11\frac{1}{9}$	**16**	$4\frac{1}{7}$
17	$2\frac{1}{2}$	**18**	$10\frac{1}{5}$	**19**	$6\frac{1}{2}$	**20**	$2\frac{1}{4}$
21	$8\frac{1}{3}$	**22**	$3\frac{1}{3}$				

9 Multiplications of fractions (page 15)

1	$\frac{12}{35}$	**2**	$\frac{25}{48}$	**3**	$\frac{3}{14}$	**4**	$\frac{4}{11}$
5	$1\frac{5}{6}$	**6**	$1\frac{1}{14}$	**7**	$3\frac{13}{24}$	**8**	$\frac{7}{10}$
9	6	**10**	$6\frac{9}{10}$	**11**	$2\frac{1}{2}$	**12**	$5\frac{5}{6}$
13	$13\frac{1}{3}$	**14**	26	**15**	4	**16**	$1\frac{3}{10}$
17	$1\frac{3}{8}$	**18**	$\frac{9}{17}$	**19**	$9\frac{1}{3}$	**20**	$5\frac{5}{8}$

10 Ratio (page 17)

1 **a** 15 **b** 210 g **c** 240 g **2** flour 1600 g, fat 400 g, sugar 400 g

3 **a** £46,875 **b** £20,000 **4** **a** 2 in 5 **b** 1 in 7 **c** 4 in 9

5 **a** 2:1 **b** 4:5 **c** 1:7 **6** **a** 2:9 **b** $\frac{2}{11}$

7 7:2:1 **8** **a** 7:4 **b** 4:7

11 Percentages (page 19)

1	80%	**2**	20%	**3**	33.33%	**4**	52.5%
5	32%	**6**	18.18%	**7**	45.71%	**8**	62.5%
9	34.28%	**10**	45.16%	**11**	81.81%	**12**	66.66%
13	26.66%	**14**	71.42%	**15**	17.5%	**16**	20.83%
17	40%	**18**	34.66%	**19**	66.66%	**20**	36.03%

12 Kitchen percentages (page 20)

1 Soup 3.42%, meat 25.14%, vegetables 9.14%, sweet 9.14%, tea and coffee 1.14%.
2 Vegetables 9.6%, meat 33.6%, dairy 16%.
3 Meat 59.17%, vegetables 14.2%, sweet 17.75%, drink 8.87%.
4 Dairy 28.73%, vegetables 13.79%, meat 57.47%.
5 Milk 5.45%, tea 11.45%, sugar 3.63%.
6 Meat 20%, vegetables 7%, sweet 5.33%.
7 Meat 20.68%, vegetables 7.24%, sweet 5.51%.
8 Increase in costs; increase in wastage; increase in portion size; pilfering.

13 Gross profit and costs (page 22)

1	75%	**2**	33.33%	**3**	66.66%	**4**	70%
5	37.5%	**6**	40%	**7**	53.33%	**8**	50%
9	46.15%	**10**	65%	**11**	56.25%	**12**	38.57%
13	96%	**14**	53.33%	**15**	43.75%	**16**	60.86%
17	54.44%	**18**	5%	**19**	60.6%	**20**	62%

Food cost percentage (page 24)

1	35.71%	**2**	**a** 33.33% **b** 66.66%	**3**	30%
4	37%	**5**	45.45%		

14 Depreciation (page 24)

1	£1,500	**2**	£1,250	**3**	25%	**4**	£1,800
5	57.14%	**6**	£1,437.50				

7 Unlikely, due to the effect of inflation.

15 Net profit (page 26)

1 10.5% **2** **a** 63.63% **b** 10% **3** 10%
4 £125 **5** **a** 40% **b** 90% **6** **a** £1.80 **b** 13.33%
7 Net loss 110% **8** **a** Yes **b** No **9** 16.5%
10 9.46% **11** **a** (i) £1,100 (ii) 8.8% (iii) £1,000 (iv) 10% **c** *A*

16 Profit and staff meals (page 28)

1 **a** (i) 66.66% (ii) 27%, (iii) 13.83%,
b (i) 70%, (ii) 30.33%, (iii) 13.83%
2 £1,060 **3** £10,800 **4** No effect

17 More about percentages (page 29)

1	£5.70	**2**	£14.25	**3**	£3.06	**4**	4.55 kg
5	0.25 litres	**6**	£1.265	**7**	£13.50	**8**	£62.04
9	£490	**10**	14 kg	**11**	37.5 litres	**12**	20 kg
13	£1,400	**14**	£0.115	**15**	£100	**16**	14 kg
17	£5,000	**18**	£0.555	**19**	3.75 kg	**20**	32 litres
21	800	**22**	18				

18 Percentage problems (page 30)

1	440	**2**	£762	**3**	£40.32	**4**	528
5	£2,750	**6**	£5.94	**7**	£198	**8**	£2,818.75
9	£25	**10**	£5,887.50	**11**	£698.50	**12**	£1,996.80
13	4.4 litres						

19 Preparing a budget (page 32)

3 **a** £4,850 **b** £5,786 **c** (i) yes (ii) £6,100

4 **a** £56,450 **b** Despite decrease in sales, certain costs will not decrease, eg rent/rates, insurance.

20 Averages (page 34)

1	**a** £3.00 **b** £20.50 **c** £7.85	**2**	£160	**3**	**a** £8.00 **b** £7.00
4	£8.50	**5**	**a** 25 **b** 25	**6**	£500
7	60	**8**	**a** £3.00 **b** mean	**9**	mode

21 Discount (page 37)

1 £36 **2** *B*, by £13.50 **3** £1,504 **4** £29.75

22 Percentage puzzles (page 38)

1	£2	**2**	£13	**3**	1.5 kg	**4**	5 litres
5	£15.625	**6**	60	**7**	£0.31	**8**	60 kg
9	£255	**10**	20 litres	**11**	90 kg	**12**	120
13	£3.00	**14**	1 litre	**15**	20	**16**	15 kg
17	£12,500	**18**	£50.00	**19**	£6.00	**20**	£18.00

23 Calculating the selling price (page 40)

1	£1.80	**2**	£5.00	**3**	£109	**4**	£2,700
5	£4.50	**6**	£301	**7**	**a** (i) £0.75 (ii) £0.96 (iii) £7.50 **b** Multiply by 3		
8	£8	**9**	£3.50	**10**	30p	**11**	£1
12	£5.85	**13**	£17.65	**15**	£2.70	**16**	£389
17	£571.42	**18**	£1	**19**	**a** 63.8% **b** £66.50		

24 Wastage (page 43)

1	40%	**2**	70%	**3**	20 kg	**4**	42 kg
5	13 kg	6	22 kg	**7**	£200	**8**	56 kg
9	*A*, by £17.75	**10**	Reliability, quality, price (discuss)				

25 VAT (page 45)

1	£14.10	**2**	£14.00	**3**	£235.00	**4**	**a** £32.90 **b** £33.60 **c** £33.04
5	£8.00	**6**	£21.00	**7**	£12.50	**8**	£1,200

26 Calculating for wines, spirits and liqueurs (page 47)

1	**a** 1000 **b** 30	**2**	**a** 50 ml **b** 105 ml	**3**	**a** 30 **b** 30 **c** 10
4	4	**5**	6	**6**	36
7	Mountain View by £18.00			**8**	£67.00
9	**a** 12 white **b** 4 red			**10**	28
11	£2.35			**12**	80

27 *Bin cards (page 49)*

1 19 kg	**2** 24 × 5 kg	**3** 29	**4** 14.25 kg
5 10 × 250 g	**6** 126		

28 *Finding the cost of food and drink used (page 51)*

1 £65	**2** £250	**3** £19,550	**4** £456
5 £1,490	**6** £1,050	**7** £665	**8** £85
9 £2,208	**10** £8,000	**11** **a** (i) £595 (ii) £575	

29 *Gross profit and the cost of sales (page 53)*

1 £5,050 **2** **a** £3,550 **b** 64.54% **3** **a** The manager
b (i) £8,525 (ii) £8,575

31 *Costing sheets (page 56)*

1

	£
Eggs	0.42
c. sugar	0.09
flour	0.046
butter	0.163
Total	0.719
portion	£0.089

2

	£
flour	0.069
c. sugar	0.045
margarine	0.090
Total	0.204
portion	£0.017

3

	£
flour	0.138
b. powder	0.055
g. sugar	0.056
suet	0.462
currants	0.200
Total	0.911
portion	£0.151

4

	£
milk	0.24
c. sugar	0.09
butter	0.081
jam	0.05
eggs	0.315
Total	0.776
portion	£0.194

5

	£
beef	3.072
c. sugar	0.013
onion	0.16
beer	0.675
Total	3.920
portion	£0.98

6

	£
lamb	1.445
potatoes	0.16
celery	0.133
b. onions	0.10
onions	0.08
leeks	0.155
Total	2.073
portion	£0.518

32 *Graphs (page 57)*

1 £20,000	**2** June	**3** Christmas and New Year trade
4 180	**5** Saturday	**6** Wednesday, Thursday
7 **a** £1,700 **b** £1,400 **c** £300		**8** £300 **9** Week 5
10 Week 9		

33 *Pie charts (page 60)*

1. Wages £5,600, insurance £480, accommodation £160, travel £160, staff meals £800.
2. Food and drink 144°, labour 90°, overheads 72°, net profit 54°.
3. Accommodation 240°, food 80°, drink and tobacco 40°.
4. Food £160,000, labour £70,000, overheads £90,000, net profit £40,000

34 *Currency conversion (page 62)*

1 £666.67 **2** 4603 pesetas **3** £21 **4** 115 000 lire

5 92 065 pesetas **6** £54.44 **7** 406 dollars **8** 27 francs
9 3700 pesetas **10** **a** £15 **b** 112.5 francs

35 Twenty-four hour clock (page 64)

1 05.00 **2** 12.25 **3** 22.00 **4** 02.10
5 11.27 **6** 12.00 **7** 23.55 **8** 15.00
9 3 a.m. **10** 5.30 p.m. **11** 12.15 a.m. **12** 4 p.m.
13 10.20 p.m. **14** 11.28 a.m. **15** 8.05 p.m. **16** 1 p.m.
17 19.05 **18** 14.40 **19** 09.50 **20** 16.50
21 Dish *A* 18.15, Dish *B* 17.35, Dish *C* 19.00, Dish *D* 18.25
22 00.49 **23** 00.02

Mixed test

Test 1 (page 66)

1 £996.03 **2** £667.69 **3** £16,032.64 **4** £1.27
5 **a** £120 **b** 26 kg **6** £37.50 **7** £39.30
8 **a** $\frac{2}{3}$ **b** $\frac{1}{6}$ **c** $\frac{3}{20}$ **9** 25 **10** 15p

Test 2 (page 66)

1 £4.29 **2** £260 **3** 30 sq m **4** £104.82
5 £4.80 **6** Meat 10.9%, vegetables 6.9%, sweets 7.27%, tea and coffee 1.27%.
7 4.372 kg **8** £1.125 **9** £104 **10** 8.75%

Test 3 (page 67)

1 **a** 66.11% **b** 10.55% **2** 21 kg **3** £66.80 **4** 7:6:13
5 £0.97 **6** 66.66% **7** £546 **8** 60%
9 15p **10** **a** £7,500 **b** £4.55

Test 4 (page 68)

1 **a** £0.44 **b** (i) £1.10 (ii) £0.66 **c** 70.66%
2 **a** £376 **b** 62.4% **3** **a** £400.50 **b** £0.88 **4** £3.25
5 £115.70 **6** £0.12

Test 5 (page 69)

1 Graph **2** **a** Meat 15.4%, vegetables 9.25%, dry goods 10.45%, beverages 3.65%
b Price rise, increase in wastage, portion control poor, pilfering.
3 **a** £0.615 **b** £1.125
4 Profit £6,000 more than budget **5** **a** 250 **b** £1.20
6 **a** 66.66% **b** 18.83% **c** 26.66% **d** 81.17%

Test 6 (page 70)

1 £15.70 **2** **a** 20 kg **b** 63.33% **c** £29.79
4 **a** £14.01 **b** £25.18 **c** £0.85 **5** 94.36%
6 **a** 55.69% **b** £1.76 **c** £1,663.20 **7** 18 cu m

Test 7 (page 70)

1 **a** £0.18 **b** £14.21 **c** £0.87 **2** 16 kg
3 **a** (i) £24,986 (ii) £35,014 **b** £804 **4** **a** £5,900 **b** £2,360
5 **a** 3025 g **b** 7.148 kg **c** 4250 ml **d** 6.035 litres
6 £16,000:£14,000

Test 8 (page 72)

1 **a** Materials (food and drink), labour, overheads. **b** (i) Overheads (ii) labour (iii) food cost (iv) overheads (v) overheads.

2 **a** 25 kg **b** £145 **3** **a** (i) 65% (ii) 60% (iii) 62.85% **b** 75.59%
4 **a** 66.66% **b** 18% **5** **a** £2.88 **b** £2.94 **c** £3.00 **6** £127.55

Test 9 (page 73)

1 **a** (i) £925 (ii) £90 (iii) 9.72% **b** Net loss
2 Increase in price charged in 5%
3 **a** (i) £415 (ii) £440 **b** (i) 68.07% (ii) 66.15%
4 **a** £1.05 **b** £0.10
5 Graph
6 Reliability, portion control, cost control, pricing uniformity.

Test 10 (page 74)

1 **a** £2.375 **b** 8.09% **2** **a** (i) £10.50 (ii) £1.75 **b** 61.11%
3 **a** 65.6% **b** 13.58% **c** 26.94% **d** 86.42%
4 59.14%

Test 11 (page 75)

1 **a** £778 **b** 56% **3** **a** 42 kg **b** 38 kg **c** *A*
4 **a** (i) £2,500 (ii) £3,150 **b** (i) £4,500 (ii) £5,150

Test 12 (page 76)

1 **a** £1,500 **b** £4,286 **c** 23.33% **2** **a** £0.42 **b** £1.05 **c** 58%
3 **a** £1,420 **b** 66.19% **c** 16% **4** £5.75

Test 13 (page 77)

1 **a** (i) *A* 67.18%, *B* 63.15% (ii) *A* 27.18%, *B* 25.26% (iii) *A* 28%, *B* 25.89% (iv) *A* 12%, *B* 12%
b *A* – larger percentage spent on labour and overheads; smaller percentage spent on food.
2 Food and drink cost could remain the same % of sales but labour and overheads would not increase in proportion to sales.
3 **a** £61 **b** 75.79% **4** **a** £36,000 **b** 62.14% **c** Graph

Test 14 (page 78)

1 **a** £90 **b** Yes, loss is £1,765 instead of £6,940 **c** 98.47%
2 **a** £19,371 **b** 61.45% **c** £1,784
3 A £2.06 B £2.94 C £5.88
5 £71.49

Multiple choice questions (page 80)

1 a	**2** d	**3** b	**4** b	**5** c	**6** a	**7** c	**8** d	**9** c
10 c	**11** d	**12** c	**13** d	**14** b	**15** c	**16** a	**17** a	**18** c

Index